Dear Bill

CINDY LONG

Dear Bill
Copyright © 2022 by Cindy Long

All rights reserved. No part of this publication may be
reproduced, distributed, or transmitted in any form or
by any means, including photocopying, recording, or
other electronic or mechanical methods, without the prior
written permission of the author, except in the case of
brief quotations embodied in critical reviews and certain
other non-commercial uses permitted by copyright law.

Tellwell Talent
www.tellwell.ca

ISBN
978-0-2288-8192-6 (Hardcover)
978-0-2288-8193-3 (Paperback)
978-0-2288-8191-9 (eBook)

Dedication

To True Love

Table of Contents

Part Two – 1953

*This letter was dated Sept. 6, but was in an envelope postmarked Aug. 7.

Preface

After the death of my mother in July of 2021, I found a stash of handwritten letters in my father's dresser drawer. They were all addressed to Dad, who had passed away the year before. I sat on the edge of their marriage bed, spreading out the old, yellowed envelopes, looking at the dates, the postmarks. Most of them were addressed to Kirkland Lake. Some of the later ones to Montréal. A couple of them weren't from my Mom, but were from Dad's mother. There were also two or three photographs. All were dated in the summer and fall of 1952 or the early fall of 1953.

All the letters had been sent from Toronto, and, with the exception of the two from Nana Long, they were love letters. After several months of wondering what to do with them, I decided to write this book.

To someone from 1950's Toronto, today would seem as alien as anything a science fiction movie could have depicted. Laser eye surgery, long-distance video chats, paying for goods by tapping a card . . . if a time traveler from 1952 heard you say, "Before I order this Bluetooth mouse for my PC online, I'm going to Google™ its ratings." they'd stare at you blankly.

A tattoo meant you were a sailor, or a concentration camp survivor. No one had envisioned the internet. If you wanted information about something, you had to go to the library. Telephones were heavy devices that sat complacently wired to the wall, and they couldn't get lost. The "golden age" of television was just beginning, and by 1960, most middle class families owned a black and white model with a heavy picture tube that sat inside a wooden frame and was controlled with knobs on the front, requiring you to get up and change channels (not that there were very many channels), and adjust an antennae that had to be positioned just right.

Small, independent movie theatres were enjoying roaring success as they were the only way to see films. If you wanted to listen to music, you went to a live concert, turned on the radio, or put a vinyl recording on a turntable. People travelled mostly by bus or train, but more and more frequently, privately owned cars were the preferred mode of long-distance travel. Highway 401 in southern Ontario was in its infancy as three small, unconnected sections of freeway and wouldn't be fully navigable from Windsor to the Québec border until 1964. Flying was still something special, and no one had been to the moon. Homosexuality was illegal and not discussed in polite company. Women did not have the same legal status as men, and the idea that a woman could act as head of a large company would have been laughed out of the boardroom. Telephone operators were essential workers.

Mom was a seventeen year old Bell telephone operator living in Toronto when she wrote the letters. She'd dropped out of high school after grade ten and started working full time. Her father and older sister, Barbara, also worked for Bell, as had her mother and eldest sister, before their marriages. She lived in East York, a former borough of the City of Toronto, in a new subdivision called Parkview Hills. Barbara (Barby), lived at home, but their oldest sister, Irene, had married in 1949 and was living in California.

Dad was a nineteen year old shoe store sales clerk who'd left school after grade nine. His father worked as a building superintendent for Imperial Oil in downtown Toronto. His three older sisters were all married, but his parents and his younger twin brothers still lived on Withrow Avenue in the Riverdale area of Toronto. Mom's family used to live a few blocks away on Albemarle Avenue. They knew each other from growing up in that neighbourhood, and had been dating for at least two years.

For reasons that were never fully disclosed to my sister and me, Dad went to Kirkland Lake in the summer of 1952 to live with his older sister, Lillian, who was married and already had two children, my cousins Ricky and Randy. Lilly's husband, my uncle Gordon, worked in the mining industry.

Dad told me once that he left Toronto because he "got in a fight". Mom told me that he "was having some trouble at home". My Aunt Barbara thought the reason might have been simply the fact that he'd been offered a job up there. What is certain is that when Dad went to Kirkland Lake, he had a sales job in Neill's Shoe Store, and that someone named Gordon had something to do with that employment. Our Aunt Lilly doesn't think her husband had anything to do with the shoe store, so perhaps it was another Gordon to whom Mom refers in her letters when she talks about Dad's work.

Not a single letter of Dad's has survived. Mom didn't save them. But Dad saved all of hers, and she wrote him several times a week.

The letters she wrote are not filled with insights and analyses of the times. They are the letters of a love-sick, seventeen year old girl pining for her absent boyfriend, and dreaming of her wedding. In them, we see glimpses of a post-war, pre-sixties Toronto that couldn't have imagined dating apps, on-line banking, or reliable contraception. Birth control was not decriminalized in Canada until 1969. When Mom wrote these letters, a woman couldn't even have a bank account without her husband's signature.

Mom was in love. It was as simple and as profound as that. She knew what she wanted, knew *who* she wanted, and she was going to make sure he was aware of that fact as often as possible. I suspect, although I don't know, that they were each other's first – and only – sexual partners. Dad was the more reserved of the two, and the only glimpse I had into his longing for Mom while they were apart was during one conversation when he told me that when Mom stepped off the train in Kirkland Lake, she was "a sight for sore eyes". But it was the way he said it that struck me, in a voice that still carried the echo of how happy he was to see her during a separation that seemed to them very long indeed.

Bill and Lois as teenagers in Toronto in 1950. Above, at the cinema. Below, in the Taylor Creek ravine. The Don Valley Parkway wasn't built until 1961. Mom and Dad would have enjoyed a far quieter, more natural environment in the east Toronto ravines than anyone born in my generation can recall.

Mom didn't mention the letters to me or my sister, but I know she discovered them herself after Dad died, because my Aunt Barbara told me that when she came to Toronto for a visit, she and Mom laughed over some of them before they were put back in the drawer.

To take a personal journey into the teenage lives of one's own parents is, I think, a rare experience. Mom must have known we'd find the letters eventually, but I'm honestly not sure how she would feel about their publication. I would be lying if I said I didn't have a moment's hesitation over assembling this book. I did. I wondered whether I was doing the right thing, taking something so private, and making it so public. In the end, it came down to throwing them away or creating this book, and this felt like the right thing to do. It's the most powerful love story I've ever read. For my sister and me, the letters explain some things, and make us wonder about others.

I wish Mom had shared their discovery with me before she passed away. There is so much I would like to ask her. She didn't, and the letters have to stand on their own, without clarification, without knowing the context of some comments, and without any editing.

PART I

The 1952 Letters

Did I Spell It Right?

July 23, 1952

Dear Bill,

I have so much to tell you, and so many questions to ask, that I hardly know how to start. Today was my day off and I went out this morning about 10:30 and didn't get home again till 9:30 this evening. This morning I went up to get that money from Doug. From there, I went down to Jean's to pick up the pills Don got for me, and from Jean's I went downtown to meet Barby. We went to the show and saw *She's Working Her Way Through College!* Had something to eat after the show and then came home.

The first thing I did was open your letter and read it. Then I got undressed and took a bath and now I can answer your letter. It's a wonder you slept so long on the train. I thought you would have trouble sleeping while you were moving like that. How did you dress and undress anyway? Can you get up any time you want in the morning?

I am coming up on the 4th of Aug. weekend, so please send my suitcase back right away. I will need it for then and that is next weekend you know. I think I will take the same train you did, but I will be taking it Fri. night. That way I will have time to go home from work and bathe, and change before I leave.

If I take the 7:00 p.m. train I will have to rush too much. Will Lillie be able to put me up for the weekend? I have Sat., Sun., Mon. off and have requested Tues. as my day off. If I don't get it, I'm going to take it anyway. I put my request in Mon. so they have plenty of time to arrange it. If there is any change in my plans I will let you know. Do you suppose someone could meet me at Swasteka because I won't be able to handle my luggage by myself (did I spell Swasteka right?)

How do you like your new job, dear? Can you walk to work or do you take a bus? What is your boss like? I hope you get along okay.

I met Bruce, the bus driver, yesterday. He said to me, "Are you married yet?" I said no, and he said, "How's Willie?" So I told him you had gone to Kirkland Lake. Boy, was he surprised! He said, "What are you going to do now?" I told him I didn't know and I really mean it, too. I am so lost without you around. We saw so much of each other when you were in Toronto. I miss you so much, dear. I wish you were back here right now. You better not come down here, because if you do, I won't let you go back. I love you so much and I hate having to be so far away from you.

Did you get the postcard I sent from Lake Simcoe? Cute, eh? Hang it up on the wall. I'll bet it would make a nice pinup.

Well, dear, it is 11:30 p.m. now so I think I will make something to eat and then go to bed. I promise to <u>be careful</u> in everything I do and whether I see you or not I am always all yours and I always will be.

All my love,

Lois

P.S. Please don't forget about sending my suitcase.

P.P.S. Did you give Lillie that earring? Oh, yes, I almost forgot. Don't forget to send that house key back to Eva.

She didn't spell it right. The town of Swastika, Ontario is just outside of Kirkland Lake. It's a junction on the Ontario Northland Railway, and in 1952, it was the place where the train stopped on its way to Cochrane from Toronto. From there, one had to take a bus into Kirkland Lake or be picked up by someone with a car.

The town was named after the Swastika Gold Mine which was staked in 1907. A swastika was originally a Sanskrit symbol for good luck. It wasn't until just prior to World War II that the symbol became associated with the Nazi Party of Germany. The provincial government tried to re-name the town "Winston" during the war, but the town's residents were having none of it. "We came up with our name first," they argued, and removed the new sign, replacing it with the old one. The government gave up. Swastika kept its name.

Photo courtesy of User P199 of Wikimedia Commons.

Mom would have gotten around Toronto by TTC. Buses and streetcars were the standard mode of transportation in the city, although private automobiles were becoming more common, and roads were becoming more congested.

TTC bus in 1954 on Yonge St. near Eglinton Ave. Photo courtesy of Toronto Public Library Digital Archive.

I first thought Mom was being a bit naïve to imagine a place like Kirkland Lake would have had public transit, but small as it was, it did have municipal bus service up until the 1970's. My cousin, Richard Woodcock, recalls it was run by McLellan Transportation, and that there were three routes. Federal-Premier serviced the north-south of town. Chaput-4ᵗʰ Street ran east-west, and there was also a bus run out to Swastika. According to Rick, they ran on the half hour and met at the bus terminal to make transfers easy. He imagines Dad would have ridden the Chaput-4ᵗʰ Street bus.

Kirkland Lake Bus in the 1950's. Copyright
William Luke. Used by permission.

The McLellan Transportation Company still exists. It operates charter buses for schools and employers in the area.

*****

When she mentioned that Don (Donald McCabe), my Dad's lifelong friend, got her some pills, I was intrigued. I thought she might have been referring to birth control pills, but those were not available in Canada until 1960, and then only for "therapeutic" purposes. Clinical trials of "the pill" didn't begin until 1956, so she clearly was referring to something else, and the mysterious pills are never mentioned again.

*****

"She's Working Her Way Through College!" (1952) was an American musical comedy that starred Virginia Mayo, Gene Nelson, and Ronald Reagan – yes, the same Ronald Reagan who would go on to become President of the United States from 1981 – 1989. The plot follows a burlesque dancer who enrolls in college and tries (unsuccessfully) to keep her job a secret from her professors and fellow students.

A Big Piece of Coconut Cream Pie

July 24, 1952

Dear Bill,

Happy Anniversary! I was so surprised when I got your phone call, I forgot to tell you then, so I'll say it now. It was wonderful to hear your voice. I didn't answer your letter after you phoned because I had to get washed, dressed, and clean up the bedroom before I went to work. I just got home from work. It is about 12:00 p.m. now. Mom just made me some tea, so I'll drink that and then finish this letter.

12:20 p.m. Just finished a cup of tea and a big piece of coconut cream pie (sound good?).

You said in your last letter that you were going out for a look at the nite life. Wasn't 11:30 p.m. kind of late? Don't think I am nagging you honey, but please be careful not to stay up too late because you'll get all worn out.

What is the nite life like up there? Is there much to do?

I was glad to hear your new boss and supervisor are nice. Especially the supervisor. I'm sure it will make a big difference to you. It's wonderful that they already think you could manage a store. I hope you get your training and get one soon even it if *is* in Timmins. Anyway, I'm willing to go anywhere in the country to live with you as long as the job has a promising future.

How do you like living with Lillie and Gord? Tell them they better take good care of you for me. Well, dear, I know this letter is a little short, but I am very tired. It is 12:40 p.m. now so I better get ready for bed.

I love you dear.

Lois.

She was definitely nagging him.

The one thing that Mom wished fervently after Dad died was that she could hear his voice again.

It was after midnight, or 12:40 a.m. when she went to bed. She always called midnight twelve p.m. I'm not sure why she used a simplified spelling pattern for the word "nite", but it's consistent throughout her correspondence.

*****

I wondered what anniversary she meant. If an engagement ring symbolized official engagement, then they weren't officially engaged, although it would appear from subsequent letters that they were committed and planning a wedding within the year. Perhaps it was the anniversary of starting to date each other? Their first kiss? Agreeing verbally to get married? We'll never know. Whatever it was, they were celebrating it each month.

I found a watch in her belongings that had an engraving on the back. It said, "Lois with love Bill 1950". Mom turned sixteen that year. Maybe the watch was a birthday gift.

*****

My sister and I found some of Mom's old China tea cups and saucers in a drawer when we were cleaning out the condo where Mom and Dad spent the last fifteen years of the lives together. Finding them instantly triggered memories for me. Nana, as we called my Mom's mother, lived with us half the year from the time of my grandfather's death in 1966 until she re-married in 1974. The other half of the year, the cold half, she lived with her eldest daughter in California. Mom and Nana regularly drank tea in the afternoon. Two teacups with matching saucers would grace the dining room table right before their favourite soap opera came on the television. They drank Red Rose brand tea. For a while, whenever you bought a package of that tea, it came with a small, china animal figurine. My sister and I were avid collectors, and tried to get as many different ones as possible, occasionally scrapping over whose turn it was to claim the precious new addition to the animal family, or deflating with disappointment when the tea box revealed a duplicate of one we both already had.

*****

I don't know how my Dad felt about staying with his sister, Lillie, and her family that summer in Kirkland Lake, but something went sour between them later on. All during my childhood, they were distant and cool with each other. I heard them say, "Hello sister." and "Hello, brother." once to each other, as if even speaking each other's names was a bit too much for them. We never visited. I was completely estranged from my four cousins. Distance was probably a big factor, but I had a feeling it wasn't the only one.

Next Time I'll Know Better

July 26/52

Dear Bill,

Received your letter when I came home from work this afternoon. I am working broken time today. Have to go back at 5:30. It is about 3:15 now so I will probably have to finish writing you when I come home again tonight.

Mom and Dad left for New Brunswick about four this morning. They woke us up to say goodbye. Didn't get to bed till about 1:00 a.m. and could hardly keep my eyes open when they left. I was supposed to get up at 7:00 so I set the alarm. Woke up about five to, and shut the alarm off, fell back to sleep, and woke up again about ten to eight. Boy, did I ever rush! Oh well, next time I'll know better.

Did you get my letter? You should have two besides the postcard. By the way, how about answering all the questions I asked in those letters? I didn't ask them just to fill up writing space you know. I expect to get some answers in your next letter! I mean it now, don't forget.

I got a letter from Dianne today so will have to answer her tomorrow. I sure am kept busy writing now.

It sounds like your new boss is keeping you busy during <u>and</u> also after working hours. Also if you have a bloated stomach next time I see you I'll know you've been drinking too much beer. Well, I guess I better stop now and get ready to go back to work.

I am all ready now, and still have some time to spare so perhaps I can finish this letter. What is the weather like in Kirkland Lake? Is it cool enough to wear a coat in the evening? I am wondering whether I will need one or not when I come up. Is someone going to meet me at the station? I asked you before, I know, but you still haven't let me know. Don't worry too much about sending my suitcase. I can always borrow Barb's. I dread the thought of coming all the way up there by myself. I hate travelling alone. I hope I will be able to get a sleeper okay because that is a holiday week and I suppose the trains will be packed. However, I'm taking that late train so it may not be too bad (I hope not, anyway).

I have to go down to Don and Jean's before I come home tonight, so I probably won't get to bed until late again. Don't have to work tomorrow so will catch up on sleep then. Will have a busy week ahead of me trying to keep house, work, and get ready to go away. Don't get paid till Fri. so can't get my train ticket ahead of time.

I have to catch the next bus so I'll close now dear.

All my love,

Lois

Steam engines were being replaced with electric diesel engines in Ontario by the 1950's. By 1960, both CN and CP had stopped using steam engines for regularly scheduled passenger and freight service, but in 1952, going between Cochrane and Toronto, Mom and Dad could have been riding on a train pulled by a steam locomotive. The line would have been operated by the Ontario Northland Railway which ran extensive passenger service, including sleeper cars.

The website for the town of Englehart has a picture of the No. 701 steam engine, and notes:

> "The 701 is the last steam locomotive to make its regular run on the Ontario Northland Rails prior the introduction of diesel use in this area. Built at Kingston in 1921, this engine retired from service in July 1957."

Which suggests that Mom and Dad were riding on a train that had a steam engine, and I think that's pretty cool.

Retired No. 701 Steam Engine on display in the town of Englehart, Ontario. (Photo courtesy of Kristina Woodcock.)

We have no pictures of Mom at work, but in 1952, she would have worked in a setting very similar to that pictured below at Bell Telephone in 1956.

"Telephone Service Across Canada", Canadian Geographic Journal, January 1956. Image credit: Michela Rosano/ Canadian Geographic. Used with permission.

Please Be Careful

July 28/52

Dear Bill,

Received two of your letters today and also my suitcase. Please thank Gord for wrapping it up so well, it is in perfect condition. Two letters came for you today. I am enclosing their contents in this letter. Please forgive me for opening them, but the address on them was already changed once and there was no room to write your new one on the envelope. Please pay that money to the finance company as soon as you can, dear. Don't let it go any longer.

I am mad at you for getting drunk the other night! Goodness knows what you told Harry about us. I don't want my life story spread all over the place! Please remember that!

Also, I am almost afraid to keep that letter you wrote the day you were sick. I know how you feel, but please be _careful_ what you write in your letters. So far I have been keeping them in a handkerchief case in one of my drawers, but tonight when I went to put your last letter away, it was at the front, and I'm sure I put it at the back. Maybe I'm too suspicious, but I think Barby was in my drawer. You probably will laugh and think I'm foolish, but did you ever stop to think what would happen if anyone read them? Please don't think I'm trying to tell you how to write your letters, dear. I love you very much and I know you don't mean to be crude, but <u>please</u> be careful – for both our sakes.

I guess I sound like a nagging old wife don't I? Well, I'm not through yet! Didn't I warn you in one of my letters about staying out too late? Apparently you ignored that part and went right ahead anyway and look what happened. You got worn out and caught the flu!

I'm not going to sympathize with you because I think it was your own damn fault! I'm not trying to stop you from having a good time, honey. To be perfectly honest with you it worries me when I think of you going out and getting drunk and then getting sick. You probably hate me now for writing and bawling you out like this. I love you too much to let you ruin your health because of a few good times. I wish I was up there with you. Then I could take care of you. As for coming up there to live, I guess you know that it is just about impossible. Even if I could get a half decent job up there. My parents would never consent. I miss you very much too, dear, but if your being up there will help us to get married and live the kind of life we want to then I'm willing to be separated from you. I know it will be well worth it.

I doubt if I will be able to come up after Aug. 16th. I won't be able to afford it. I only wish I could. I would give almost anything to be able to come.

It is 11:15 p.m. now so I think I'll get washed and go to bed. I'm 6 – 12 tomorrow, but have to get up early so I can do a washing and clean the house.

I am very lonely without you, dear, and I'll be so happy to see you this weekend. I promise to be prepared for a lot of loving.

All my love,

Lois

P.S. I'm sorry but I don't have enough room to enclose your other letter. It is just another book advertisement from McGraw Hill. If you do want it, let me know and I will send it in another letter.

PREMIER FINANCE CORPORATION LTD.

100 ADELAIDE WEST, TORONTO — EM. 6-8811
(BUDGET OFFICE)

We have not received payment of your overdue account at

SEL'S MENS WEAR

If you cannot go to the store, kindly mail the payment direct to us within the next two or three days.

If convenient, please telephone EM. 6-8811 and make suitable arrangements.

Mr. William Long,
108 Withrow Avenue,
TORONTO.

THANKING YOU FOR YOUR IMMEDIATE ATTENTION

The overdue bill notice Mom enclosed with this letter.

We'd love to know what it was that Dad wrote that gave her so much anxiety! (For the record, my aunt Barbara swears she never read the letters.)

A Hard Boiled Egg, Rolls, and Tea

10:15 p.m.

Aug. 6/52

Hello, Dear,

Hope you got my wire ok. This is going to be a short letter. I am writing it in bed & as soon as I am finished I am going to switch out the light & go to sleep. (Have to get up at 6 tomorrow.)

The trip back home was nice. I slept very good. Got up about 7:30 and had breakfast. All I had was tomato juice, a hard boiled egg, rolls and tea. It cost me $1.05. Isn't that awful? We got in Toronto about 9:20 a.m. I sent you wire and went straight home. I was still tired when I got home, so I went to sleep for about 3 hrs. Then got up & did some shopping Thurs. night as I am going to the Royal Alex to see the stage play *Goodnight Ladies.* It is supposed to be real good. I'm going with Shirley Clarke, one of the girls from work. We are both 7 – 4 on Thurs. (Ugh) What a thought! Makes me tired to think of it.

Received more postcards from Mom & Dad today. They expect to be home this coming Sat. Sure will be glad to see them. Especially Mom – I can't stand my own cooking any longer.

I guess that's all for now dear. Please write soon. I love you very much.

Lois.

Goodnite Ladies *ran from August 4 – 16 that year at the Royal Alexandra Theatre in Toronto. It's a silly little comedy, originally performed in the 1920's under the title* Ladies' Night. *The convoluted plot involves some friends who try to cure the anxieties of a man who is embarrassed by immodestly dressed women by taking him to a masquerade event in drag, but they inadvertently end up in a "Turkish bath" on "ladies' night". Apparently, even its harshest critics had to admit it was pretty funny at times.*

The Royal Alex, as it's always been known, has a colourful history in Toronto.

Photo courtesy Wikimedia Commons.

The theatre opened in 1907, financed by a group of wealthy Toronto businessmen. It was the first in the world to have a form of air conditioning, which involved keeping ice in tanks below the floors. Edward "Honest Ed" Mirvish purchased it in 1963 and spent probably around half a million dollars to restore it to its former splendor.

Allan Levine wrote in Toronto: Biography of a City:

> "In typical Mirvish style, the refurbished Royal Alex had a huge marquee sign with more than a thousand flashing lights...Since then, the theatre has showcased a bevy of popular Broadway plays and musicals attracting large audiences."

In 2018, the restored theatre had around 45,000 annual ticket subscribers, but in 1952, it was 45 years old and not aging well. Mom and her friends would have sat in what seemed like a decrepit building with peeling wallpaper, faded carpets, and uncomfortable seats. Its elegance could not be denied, but without Mirvish's purchase and restoration, it probably would have been torn down.

The Mirvish project re-vitalized Toronto's King Street, attracting other businesses to the area once again.

I'm Nagging You Again, Aren't I?

Aug. 12/52

Dear Bill,

Received your letter last night when I got home from work. I was so glad to hear from you. It seems like ages since I last saw you – yet it's only a week. I wanted to answer your letter last night, but I was going out so I didn't get around to it. Are you still coming down on Labour Day weekend? I have that weekend off. It sure would be wonderful if you could make it. I miss you more too – since I saw you last weekend.

Mom & dad came home from their vacation last Fri. They weren't supposed to arrive until Sat. but they made it sooner than they expected. They left N. Brunswick Thurs. morning. They got as far as Quebec City and stayed there Thurs. nite. Then they left Quebec at 6:00 a.m. Fri. morning & arrived in Toro. about 11:00 p.m. so they made very good time didn't they? They had a wonderful time. Stayed in N. Brunswick most of the time, but visited all three of the Maritimes. Took a tour of P.E.I. but didn't go far past the border when they went into Nova Scotia. On the way to N. Brunswick they stopped in Bar Harbour, Maine. The mayor there knew

Ruth & he took them around the place in his Cadillac & they spent the nite in his home. He also took them for a lobster dinner and before Mom & Dad left he gave them a book on Bar Harbour. It tells the whole history of the place and was autographed personally by the author. They brought back tons of little souvenirs. I picked out one for you, honey. It is from a place called The Rocks at Hopewell Cape, N. Brunswick. It's a blue china fish with a great big mouth opened wide. It is hollow inside. We thought it made a cute ash tray. That's the main reason I picked that one for you. For myself I picked one of those crystal balls. You know the kind I mean – it has a picture of the Chateau Frontenac in Quebec. When you shake it, it looks like it's snowing.

A postcard came for you the other day. It is from your brothers at the falls. I'm enclosing it in this letter. Don't forget to send that money to the finance co. and also the key to Eva. In your next letter I want to hear that you've done both those things.

Please tell Gord that I have 2 of Mickey Spillane's books for him. I'm going to try to wrap them today and send them up. I also have another one to send but Bol Dixon has it right now. I'll send it when he's finished with it.

Some nite this week I'm going to babysit for Jean. She & Don want to see that picture, *King Kong.* It started downtown last Fri. I want to see it, too, but don't know if I'll get around to it. Some say it's real good & others didn't like it at all.

By the way, did you know you addressed my last letter Lois Forth 201 Parkview Hills Cr.? Don't I rate a "Miss" in front of my name? And what in heavens happened to the "k" in Parkview Hills? The postman put it in pencil. You must have really been feeling terrible. Anyway my proper address is at the top of the letter. Please address them that way after this – so there! I'm nagging you again aren't I?

I was sorry to hear you had a cold, dear. I also caught one. I had a terrible sore throat at first and then on top of that the cold went to my head. Now it has moved to my chest. I can't seem to shake it. I really felt rotten this past weekend. To top it off I had to work both Sat. & Sun.

Have you thought any more about going out in the truck with Harry in the fall? It might be worth your while. You would be making more & would be able to save <u>much</u> more.

Mr. Medill has promised to get his typewriter from school when it opens again in the fall. Barby is going to teach me typing. As soon as I can work up a <u>very</u> good speed I'm going to quit the Bell and get a better paying job. I'd like to get one as a Switchboard-Receptionist or Switchboard-Typist. Oh well, I'll just have to wait & see how things turn out. Who knows? Maybe I'll make a poor typist.

I didn't mean to make this letter so long. It wasn't supposed to go over three pages, but I've been rambling on & now I've started a fourth.

Did you hear who was chosen as Miss Canada? Marilyn Reddick! I'm enclosing her picture and the write up that was in the Globe & Mail. Gee – this letter is going to be so thick – you may have to pay more postage on it.

Have you got any postcards up there with a picture of the store in them? Look around & if you can find any send them down.

It's 11;45 now. I haven't really been writing all that time though. I was interrupted 2 or 3 times. I'm 5 – 11 today & off tomorrow. I'm going to wrap Gord's books now. Then go out to Taylors & send them – also have to buy some cigarettes. Mom brought back some Chesterfields from Bangor, Maine, but I don't like them. They're packed very loosely and of course no cork tips.

Well, honey bubbles, lunch is just about ready so I guess I'd better go.

All my love,

Lois

How many versions of this movie have been made? A lot, is the answer, but in 1952, it was just a re-release of the original 1933 film starring Fay Wray, Robert Armstrong, Bruce Cabot, and, of course, Kong himself. It was a commercial success, inspiring more monster movies, most notably Godzilla.

****

At first, I thought Bar Harbour, Maine, was an odd place to go through on the way to New Brunswick from Toronto, until I remembered that my grandparents frequently travelled stateside. My grandmother had some good friends named Ed and Irene Flavin living in Syracuse, New York. Mom's parents probably crossed the border at Niagara Falls. They also might have crossed at the Thousand Islands Bridge east of Kingston. They would have been visiting the small, resort community of Bar Harbour only five years after a wildfire devastated much of the island on which it lies.

****

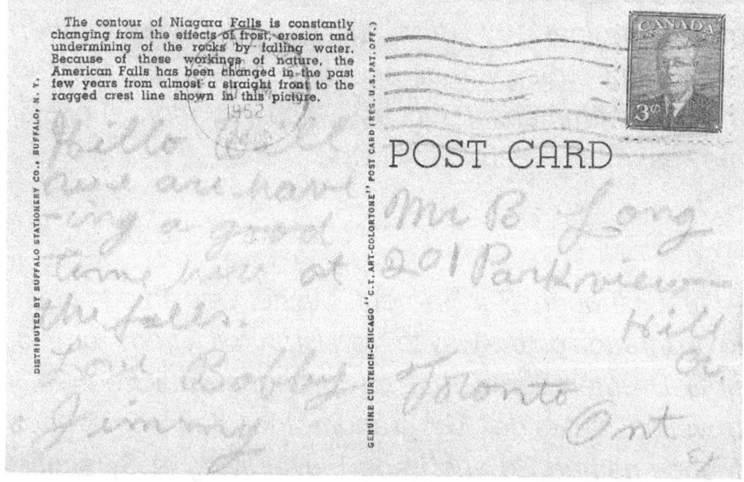

Dad was already twelve years old when Jim and Bob, his younger twin brothers, were born. Up until then, he'd enjoyed status as the youngest, and the only boy in the family, the same as his maternal uncle and namesake William Lalonde had done a generation before. I don't know if my grandmother was embarrassed by a pregnancy when she was in her early forties, or if she

just enjoyed messing with people's heads, but when her belly started to swell, she reportedly told everyone she had a tumour. Mom seemed to enjoy spending time with "the boys" as she called them. There are several pictures of Mom and Dad with the twins, and it always looks to me as if Mom was playing the part of a big sister to them.

*****

Marilyn Reddick might have been the daughter of family friends, a distant relative, or someone they knew from school or the neighbourhood, although the clipping said she was from Agincourt. She was around the same age as them, 18, and the article said she had been the runner-up in the Miss Toronto beauty pageant a few weeks earlier. I originally thought this was my mother's cousin, Marilyn, but the surname is wrong, and my aunt confirmed it wasn't her.

Marilyn Dolores Reddick – winner of Miss Canada 1952.
Used by permission. The Globe and Mail/CP

*****

Mickey Spillane's novels, often featuring detective Mike Hammer, were the testosterone-based version of cheap romance novels. They were crime and detective stories that pushed the boundaries of what was considered decent at the time, featuring more sex and graphic violence than similar contemporary titles in the genre. The covers were often lurid and sensational. Literate teenage boys devoured them. The critics might not have been impressed, but Spillane's books sold over 225 million copies internationally.

*****

Mom mentions smoking more than once in her letters. Chesterfield cigarettes were among the first brand to target women as potential smokers with their advertising. The ad below is from 1941. Both my Mom and her sister thought smoking was pretty avant-garde at the time. Mom didn't quit until she was pregnant with me in 1963. She told me that the doctor suggested to her that smoking could be harmful to the baby. My childhood was full of people smoking, despite the fact that both parents had quit. Other relatives smoked in cars we drove in; people smoked in cinemas, restaurants, office waiting rooms, the school staffroom, even airplanes. There was no escaping it. I worked briefly at a bingo hall as a teenager, and would come home late reeking of cigarette smoke that lingered in my bedclothes, my closet, and probably my lungs.

Image courtesy of First Versions, www.firstversions.com

A Bad Case of the Blues

Aug. 13/52

Dear Bill,

I was so happy to get your letter today. I almost burst into tears. Isn't that silly? I have a very bad case of what they call the blues. Mom & dad left for Syracuse N.Y. this AM about 9;30, so I'm all alone again. It's a beautiful day here – warm, but not real hot – the kind of day that makes you want to go somewhere and <u>do</u> something. Yet when I stop to think of it, what can I <u>do</u>? – absolutely nothing! Sometimes I think I'll go crazy if I don't tell someone how I feel. That's why I'm telling you, dear, because I know you'll understand. I suppose I shouldn't feel so sorry for myself, but I just can't help it! There is still some housework to be done, but so far all I've done is play records and smoke cigarettes. Maybe I haven't done the housework because I know when I've finished that, I'll have nothing else to do. I could go out for a walk and tell everyone what a nice day it is and how wonderful it is to be alive, but the majority of them would think I was crazy. I know all this kind of talk must be depressing to you so I won't say anymore.

Two other letters came today – both from the finance co. I am enclosing them in this letter. I was glad to hear you're going to pay off all your debts. Don't get too involved with the credit union. Remember you still have to pay it back and it won't be as easy as it was to get it. If you borrow the money for my ring from them, do you think you would be able to pay them back and also save money for our marriage? I guess you could though. $16.66 a month works out to about $4.25 a week. I would love to have my ring of course, but I think the decision should be entirely your own. I think it's a good idea but I don't want you to be swayed by anyone's judgment but your own.

I am sorry dear, but I couldn't come up this weekend as it is too late for you to send the money. Next weekend I have to work on Sat. so I couldn't come then either. I want to see you again soon though so <u>please please</u> come down on Labour Day weekend. Why don't you use the money you would have had to send for my train fare to pay off your debt to Lilly? It would be better to pay her what you owe before you borrow more. How much did you borrow? And don't forget to answer these questions in your next letter!

From the sound of your letter you actually do enjoy your job up there. It's just swell that you do, too. I was hoping you wouldn't get fed up with it like you did the others. I'm going to phone Agnew's next week & see if your money is there. I could use whatever sum they have for you. I shouldn't talk to you about debts I guess because right now I owe about $46 on Simpson's account. So that takes care of my next 2 paychecks. I'm taking half of the sum out of this Fri. pay & the other half out of my next pay. I'll still have some left over to put in the bank. It's about time I started saving, too.

You tell Gord to quit putting bad ideas in your head or I won't send him any more of Mickey Spillane's books.

It's good your cold has started to break. Mine has, too. Did you go to a doctor? Just a minute. I want to light a cigarette. Mom says I don't eat enough or get the proper sleep and that's why I can't shake this cold. But when I'm home by myself I never bother eating. Sometimes I only have one meal a day. I never feel real hungry though.

As long as I don't I guess it's ok. I don't think I've lost weight but then I don't really know. I haven't weighed myself since before you went away.

How are Randy and Ricky? Have they still got that crazy ball I bought them or have they broken it? I didn't think they would be able to keep it in one piece for very long. Say hello to Gord, your boss, and tell him I said not to work you too hard. Did you know that Sun Aug 10 was Don's birthday? I forgot. Jean gave him a nice camera. It's a Brownie with a flash attachment. Did you try out your camera yet? Why don't you? If the pictures turn out send some down to me. I'd love to have some of the folks up there. If they don't turn out, borrow Lilly's camera & take some & send them. That's an order! (ha ha)

Well, I think I'll finish the housework, get washed & dressed & then go out & mail this letter. Goodbye for now dear.

All my love,

Lois.

P.S. I love the printing.

P.P.S. Just heard on the radio that they're going to tear down Yonge St. arcade and put a parking station in its place.

This is the first time she mentions the ring, but it won't be the last.

I looked up weekly wages and salaries in Canada in 1952. What I found was that men were earning anywhere from about $34 - $60 a week, depending on the industry. Sales clerk jobs often depended at least partly on commissions. Insurance and finance jobs earned closer to $50 a week, and Dad did eventually end up as an insurance salesman. If we assume Dad was making $50 a week, $4.25 as a weekly payment on an engagement ring would have been just under 10% of his salary.

*****

Department store credit became widespread in Canada in the 1940's. Since it was difficult, if not impossible, for a single woman to get a credit card from a bank, department store credit was a popular option. Mom probably had to get her father to co-sign for it, though. Simpson's was still offering store credit cards in the 1990's. Every time I made a purchase, the staff member would ask me if that was on my Simpson's card, and when I said no, they'd ask if I had one, and then if I wanted one. Every time.

*****

Brownie Cameras were all the rage in the 1950's. As a kid, I used to fool around with one that my Dad had kept from that era. They had simple controls, used Kodak film, and were priced within reach of the average consumer. Especially helpful was the invention of the built-in flash in 1957. Prior to that, you had to have a flash attachment that took single use flash bulbs. The bulbs were really hot right after they went off. I remember burning my finger on one when I tried to remove it before it had cooled.

©copyright Nicholas Middleton. Used with permission.

*****

I'm inferring from this letter that Dad worked at Agnew Surpass right before going up to Kirkland Lake. Agnew Surpass was a popular shoe store that would sometimes take out full page ads in the Toronto newspapers. Founded in 1879, it was the largest chain of shoe stores in Canada before it went bankrupt in 2000. My friend and I would go to a local mall in the 1970's to shop, and like every other mall, it had an Agnew Surpass shoe store. I'm sure I helped their bottom line from time to time. I always thought the name was odd. It reminded me of the phrase "army surplus", and sounded wrong to my ear because of that similarity.

*****

The Yonge Street Arcade in Toronto was a four-storey indoor shopping space built in 1884. It is considered to have been Canada's first indoor shopping mall.

The Yonge Street Arcade, circa 1885. Courtesy of the Toronto Public Library.

The exterior of the arcade had a unique, visual splendor. Designed by English architect Charles A. Walton, it was intended to resemble, in both form and function, the 19th century glass-roofed galleries of Europe. Merchants were eager to lease space which would allow them some competition with the three retail giants dominating the Toronto downtown at the time – Eaton's, Simpson's, and The Golden Lion. The Golden Lion closed its doors only fourteen years later, in 1898, but Eaton's and Simpson's went on to become national retail giants.

The Yonge Street Arcade used to advertise that it sold "nothing over $25". After years of neglected maintenance *and two fires, it was demolished in 1954, and did indeed serve briefly as a paved parking lot. In 1960, a ten-storey office building that remains to this day was erected on the site at 137 Yonge Street between Richmond and Adelaide. The new building originally had some retail shops at ground level, but currently houses a fitness center.*

*****

Most of Mom's letters were written in ink on very plain sheets of notepaper about 20 X 13 cm. The occasional letter was written on colourful, scented stationery, like this next one.

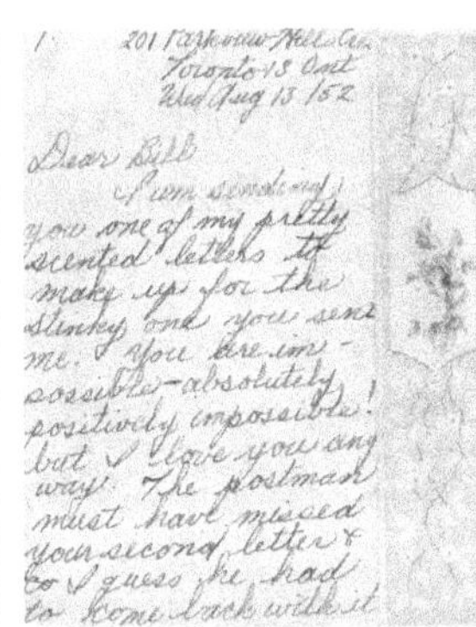

Stinky Letter

Aug. 13/52

Dear Bill,

I am sending you one of my pretty scented letters to make up for the stinky one you sent me. You are impossible – absolutely positively impossible! But I love you anyway. The postman must have missed your second letter & I guess he had to come back with it because it didn't come with the first one. I just went to see if there was any bread in the milk chute & there was your letter! Was I surprised! I feel a lot better now – not half as blue. Enclosed are some more newspaper clippings. They're from the Star. Thought you might like to read them.

I haven't got much to say in this letter because I just finished writing one. I'm sitting here munching on raw carrots. All of a sudden I had a great <u>craving</u> for them. (ha ha) They're from our vegetable garden and they taste very good. Anyway they're not fattening & they're supposed to be good for the eyes. Maybe they'll help me to keep my eyes open tomorrow morning. I'm 7 – 4 tomorrow & have to get up at 5:00 AM. That's all for now "sweetie pie". Don't let your dreams keep you awake nites.

All my love

Lois

Did Dad actually send Mom a letter that smelled bad, or was she referring to the tone of his letter? We'll never know.

*****

Bread in the milk chute. I do get that reference. At the house we had in Parkview Hills in East York – Mom and Dad eventually purchased our family home in the same neighbourhood in which she had been living when she wrote him those letters – there was a box built into the wall of the house next to the side door. You could open it from the outside or the inside of the house. On the inside, it had a little lock on the door. There was still door-to-door milk delivery at the time we lived there in the early 70's. Al from Sealtest Dairies would come along in a truck. Mom would leave the order in the milk box for him, along with the money, and he'd leave milk, butter, or whatever she ordered. In the 50's, there was both milk and bread delivery, and the bread man would leave the loaf in the same box. My grandmother recalled that they used to come around in a horse-drawn cart. I also remember a fruit and vegetable vendor, and a man who offered sharpening services – garden tools, axes, knives, whatever. That one would play a distinctive, repetitive little melody over a loudspeaker as his truck cruised slowly through the residential streets, stopping only if flagged down. None of this continued into the 1980's.

*****

Mom included more clippings about Marilyn's big win with this letter, this time from the Toronto Star newspaper. Until the day they died, Mom and Dad continued to subscribe to both large dailies, and eventually the Toronto Sun. Mom would occasionally send me clippings from one or the other that she thought I'd find interesting (or that she thought would improve my life in some way – Dad wasn't her only project).

YES! I Do Want My Ring

Aug. 18/52

Dear Bill,

First of all, I want to clear up a little misunderstanding. In my last letter, I did not say I didn't want you to borrow the money for my ring from the Credit Union. Apparently that's what you thought I meant, though. In fact, I told you I thought it was a good idea, but that I didn't want you to start anything you couldn't finish. You've asked me to tell you what I really think & I can't tell you anymore than what I've already said. YES! I do want my ring! As long as you feel you can manage it, then it's perfectly ok with me.

It's too bad you can't get the Sat before Labour Day off. Then maybe you could leave Fri nite & get here Sat. We would have more time with each other then. Why don't you ask Gord if you can have it off? I don't suppose he would be able to spare you though. Anyway, it's a nice thought.

Sat Sept 20th I am going to Buffalo for the day with some of the girls from the office. Every year they arrange a trip. They leave early in the a.m. & come back about 3:30 a.m. Sun. The fare is $6.80 & that includes a hotel room, tips, and a visit to the Towne Casino. I'm saving the money in bits & pieces & will soon have enough. The kids usually have a swell time & I'm sort of looking forward to it.

Mom & Dad came home from Syracuse tonite about 8:00 p.m. Aunt Irene came with them. She brought me a pair of green bed sheets & pillow cases to match. They're really smart. I think you'll like them. Mom & Dad brought Barby & I each a nylon blouse, metal skirt hangers, nylon net stockings, nail brushes & some lipstick that is <u>not</u> supposed to come off. You better hurry down here real soon so I can try it out!

Why have you changed your mailing address? Is it because you get delivery to the store? Did Gordy get the books I sent him?

Your news about returning to Toro is wonderful. I only wish it could be sooner. Christmas will be a long time coming <u>this</u> year with you so far away from me. Do you still plan to go out in the truck with Harry this fall? If you do maybe you could squeeze in a trip to Toro. (ha ha fat chance I know) Have you shaved your moustache off yet? I won't let you kiss me again until you do. (ha ha again)

I forgot to tell you we didn't go to the Royal Alex that nite because we got out of work at 4:00 p.m. & the evening performance didn't start until 8:30 p.m. That left us with too much time to kill so we went to the show and saw *We're Not Married"*.

Sat nite Barby & I got dressed to kill & went to The Town & Country Club for dinner. Wasn't sure whether or not they would serve me a drink but the waiter put a cocktail menu down in front of me so I ordered a Gin Fizz. It was very good. After our drink we went and got our dinner. You just walk to the back of the room and pick out whatever you like and put it on your plate. The things you can't reach the chef puts on for you. They have all sorts of things. It is buffet style. You can take as much as you like & go back as many times as you like. All it will cost is $1.90. Your drink & dessert is extra, also the cocktails. It cost us $2.25 each. After dinner we went to the Odeon Toro. & saw *All Because of Sally.*

Sat. I bought that record *Auf Wiedersehn* by Vera Lynn & Barby bought 2 more of Mario Lanza's records. She has played each record about twelve times & I'm just about going crazy. I've hardly had a chance to play my own. Oh well, Tues is my day off & she won't be around. I'll play them then.

Well honey, it's getting late so I better go to bed. Goodnite dear. I love you.

Lois

Image courtesy of Torontoist.

The Town & Country in the Westminster Hotel had opened only three years previously in 1949. One ad in the Globe & Mail newspaper assured potential customers that it was the place "where dishes from all over the world await your approval". An all-you-can-eat buffet was a new style of dining experience for staid Toronto. Marketed as exotic and adventurous, but elegant, it would have been irresistible to Mom and her sister. I'd love to see how they looked when they were "dressed to kill".

*****

I did a quick internet search for the movie "All Because of Sally" and nothing came up except a 1952 MacLean's magazine rating that stated it was a comedy and gave it a rating of "fair". A December 8, 1952 issue of the Sherbrooke Daily Record, alongside articles about how allied planes were "plastering communist targets" in North Korea, advertises a movie by that title, but goes on to describe it as "the story of Sally and Ste. Anne". There was a popular 1952 movie called "Sally and Ste. Anne" for which I could find several references, so I'm left wondering if the Sherbrooke newspaper mistook one film for the other.

"We're Not Married", another American romantic-comedy with a star-studded cast, left a far bigger footprint in the cinematic sands. Several couples find out they're not legally married because the justice of the peace who married them wasn't officially a J.P. at the time he performed the ceremonies. The film revolves around their reactions. (I'm starting to think rom-coms were all the rage in 1952.)

*****

*The Town Casino is now called The Town Ballroom. In the 50's, it billed itself as "the largest nightclub between Chicago and New York City" and was **the** place to be in Buffalo between 1940 and 1960 with three shows a night and lots of big names. It's rumoured that Frank Sinatra used to enjoy it. People from Toronto would cross to the other side of the lake via Niagara Falls because American laws were far more relaxed when it came to liquor and fun. As a young adult, I had a hard time understanding my parents' fondness for trips to the*

U.S.A., but I didn't grow up in fifties Toronto where, as my Dad used to say, they "rolled up the sidewalks by nine p.m.". Even after Ontario relaxed its liquor laws and Toronto had more to offer in the way of entertainment and nightlife, my parents stuck to their old habits, and visited Buffalo when they wanted to go to a casino.

*****

I was familiar with Dame Vera Lynn, the popular World War II singer with the famous hits "We'll Meet Again" and "The White Cliffs of Dover". However, I'd never heard of Mario Lanza. Turns out he was a huge superstar in 1951, three years before Elvis Presley came on the scene, and nearly as well-known as Presley would come to be. A trained opera singer, Lanza was both a film star – The Great Caruso being possibly his top grossing film – and a recording artist. He died young, only 38 years old, which might explain why I hadn't heard of him.

Toronto Will Seem a Little Dull

Aug. 20/52

Dear Bill,

I came home from work about 1 ½ hrs ago but didn't have time to answer your letter until now. Aunt Eva & Uncle Bill are down from North Bay for a couple of days. I didn't know they were here until I got home. We have been sitting here talking ever since. I really haven't much to say in this letter. Haven't been doing anything interesting. I went to a shower for one of the girls after work tonite & I am so tired. I didn't sleep at all last nite. I don't know what was the matter with me. I laid awake all night. Aunt Irene was sleeping in Barby's bed & she said she knew I wasn't sleeping cause I kept her awake tossing & turning. My eyes are hurting & the nerve in the right one keeps jumping. Guess I'm just a nervous old wreck, eh?

Sounds like you had a terrific time in Rouyn. You'll probably be raring to go back after Labour Day weekend. Toro will seem a little dull. After all, you can't get into the hotels & bars here you know. Jean & Don want us to go down to this place for dinner when you come. How are you coming? By train? I sure wish you could get Sat off too. Please don't wait around after you get to Toro. Come straight to my place. Mom & Dad said they don't care what time you come. The quicker the better. I guess they're tired of me mooning around the house like I had lost my last friend. I wish you could get the money for my ring before you come. Then we could pick one out. <u>If</u> you arrive Sat and <u>if</u> you had the money. But I guess there's not much chance of that. You can't blame me for trying, though, can you?

Your idea about meeting in North Bay is a good one. I mentioned it to Mom & Aunt Eva said, "You can stay at our place if you like.' Naturally, Mom thought that was a grand idea.

Would that course you mentioned cost much money? Don't forget we have to save. I have my wedding dress all picked out. All that has to be changed will be the neckline. Otherwise, it's perfect. The dress will be made of course, but what I mean is I have the style & fabric chosen. April is only 8 months away you know. That's not very far off when you stop to consider all the planning that has to be done. I even know what kind of flowers I want. It will be around Easter Time so I'm going to have white Easter lilies & Lilly-of-the-valley. See how far ahead I've planned & I haven't even got you hooked properly yet.

Well, honey, that's all for tonite.

All my love,

Lois

I think getting him "hooked" depended on getting the ring.

This ad was circulating in 1952.

Rouyn, now called Rouyn-Noranda, is just over the provincial border in Québec. It's about an hour's drive from Kirkland Lake, and was the happening place to go in the 1950's for young people who lived nearby. The age of majority in Ontario was 21, but in Québec, it was

18, and they were lax about checking ID. My cousin, Richard, remembers two bars there – the Moulin Rouge and the Radio. Both were open until 3 a.m. There were no stand-up bars in Ontario before 1960, and Toronto's liquor laws were some of the strictest anywhere. As Mom felt obliged to point out, Dad couldn't get into bars in Toronto since he was only nineteen.

For a boy from "Toronto the Good", Rouyn must have seemed like Paris.

*****

When my Mom mentions Bill and Eva, she's talking about her father's older brother, William, and his wife Eva. Our Uncle Bill had purchased land on Callander Bay, just south of the city of North Bay. He constructed a set of cabins and ran Green Road Cottages for years. They were rented mainly to people looking for a fishing vacation. Green Road Cottages still exists, fully renovated and under new ownership.

The North Bay connection was a strong one in our family. Mom's German grandfather had immigrated from the U.S. to Bracebridge, Ontario in the late 1800's to work on the railway. Some of his children moved both south to Toronto, and north to the Parry Sound and North Bay areas where their descendants still live.

Don't Believe Everything You Read

Aug. 21/52

Dear Bill,

Well, here I am all curled up in a corner of the couch – trying to make myself as comfortable as possible while I answer your letter. How do you like living the carefree life of a bachelor? Can you eat your own cooking without turning green? Anyway, if you can't eat it, there's always Lucky. She'll eat anything, eh? Tomorrow nite I'll find out what kind of a cook Jean is. I'm going to sit with Larry while she & Don go to the show so she asked me to go down to their place for dinner. Larry is getting to be real cute – especially when he smiles. I usually go down to see Jean once a week. Most of the time I go in the PM while Don is still at work. We sit around and talk and drink (tea of course). Jean doesn't have any trouble with Larry now at all. She is still breastfeeding him, but is also giving him pablum. She doesn't have to feed him at 10:00 PM anymore so that means he sleeps from 6:00 PM right through until 6 in the AM.

I had a letter from Diane on Monday. She says she's coming down to Toro. this fall. I hope she comes to our place to stay while she is here. I would like to see her again.

We're going to have a full house on Labour Day weekend. Aunt Irene, Uncle Ed, Ted & Dorelle <u>may</u> be coming down. If so, they'll be staying here, too. But we don't know for sure if they're coming. The only guest we're sure of is you (thank goodness). I am going to meet you at the station if you come by train – and you can count on being plenty embarrassed, moustache and all!

By the way, don't believe everything you read in those magazines. Sometimes they can do you much more harm than good. Absence certainly does make the heart grow fonder, dear. At least, in my case it does. I love you very much and being away from you like this makes me realize how important you are to me and how much I need you. You just keep loving me and everything will be fine, okey dokey dear?

Goodnite honey,

All my love,

Lois

They believed their love would hold their world together. And it did. My sister and I tried more than once to open a conversation with our parents about planning for their elder years, to attempt to get some sense of what their wishes were should they become less able to care for themselves. As soon as we'd bring up finances and what they'd be able to afford, they would brush us off. My Dad, in particular, would often repeat the line. "We're not worried about it. We'll live on our love."

****

Mom's need for Dad never diminished. After they installed a swimming pool, we used to joke that he was her "pool boy". He spent many hours keeping it clean, but rarely used it, and never when others were around. Apart from a few lengths early some mornings, his interactions with the pool were confined to maintenance, and serving drinks poolside while Mom lounged for hours on hot, summer days, often with her friend, Betty, or her sister Barb, if she happened to be visiting. As they aged, Dad continued to take care of Mom, eventually taking over most of the household chores, including meal preparation. His last, emphatic instruction to my sister and me was, "Take care of your mother!!"

****

Mom had been friends with Jean McCabe since childhood. They remained friends up until Mom's death, although the Covid-19 crisis and Jean's residence in a nursing home made visiting difficult in the last two years of Mom's life. They spoke on the phone regularly, however, and it was clear that they both still valued the friendship highly.

****

Lucky was a black and white spaniel that my cousin recalls being around when he was very small, but I have no idea who Diane was, nor Ted and Dorelle.

Lovely Anniversary Present

Dear Bill,

Your phone call was a lovely anniversary present. It was the second one that day for me. I woke up Sun. morning with stomach cramps & I felt just rotten. (Three guesses why.) Sun. afternoon we decided to drive out to Mary's. She has a nice television set. It's a Crosley and the reception is good. We took some pictures while we were there. They should be ready sometime this week. You can see them on Sun. and if you want any copies I'll get them done & send them to you. Also, I'll try to get some taken of me in that suit. Right now my suit is dirty. It's going to the cleaners tomorrow. I'm going to buy a couple of films so we can take some pictures while you are here, too.

I requested next Tues. as my day off. If they don't give it to me I'll stay off anyway. So now you won't have to go back until Tues. nite. You can take the 7:00 PM train & you'll get up there in time to go to work Wed. AM. If you have a berth you shouldn't be too tired. Will you have enough money for my ring? What I mean to say is, did you borrow any from the Credit Union? If so, then we could look at rings on Tues. I'm not anxious to get it or anything am I? (ha ha) Even if you don't have a lot of money maybe we could put a down payment on one – I hope.

Have enclosed a small newspaper clipping. I cut it out of the Star. That incident occurred while Mom & Dad were in Syracuse. Some friends of Aunt Irene's happened to live right near there and they saw it all. In fact, they enjoyed it so much that when dinner time came, they ate in a big hurry, grabbed their dessert in their hands & rushed back out to the porch to watch the fun. They told Aunt Irene about it & she told Mum & Dad. Then after they came home, Mom read the article about it in the paper. When the kids saw the policeman come around the corner, they threw the sign into the bushes and ran like sixty.

Your writing so much about your work doesn't bore me in the least honey. I like to hear about it. I'm glad that you really enjoy your work. That's half the battle, you know. Also I think you would be perfectly justified in mentioning Joyce's sales manner to Gord. After all, if she could adopt a better attitude it would certainly help the sales.

The poem you enclosed in your letter was beautiful. Where did you find it? You must be doing some heavy reading.

It's too bad you're going to keep your moustache <u>dear</u>. I hope it doesn't tickle.

I phoned Don tonite. He said Jean is feeling better although she's still in bed. He had to stay off work so he could take care of her & the baby. She should be up in a few days though. Don said he had to change a dirty diaper today & it almost made him sick to his stomach. I told him he should breathe through his mouth & not his nose. He agreed wholeheartedly & said the next time he would be sure to do it that way.

I also phoned Agnew's about your money today. The new mgr. said that the spiff money wasn't in yet. He told me to give him my phone number & he would call me when it came. He was very nice about it.

Doug's store is really supposed to be something. I haven't seen it yet. Am enclosing part of the ad from the paper. Maybe we can drop in next Tues. if we go downtown.

Well, honey I guess I better do my hair up and go to bed. I couldn't sleep last nite. There was a mosquito in our bedroom & it kept buzzing around my ears. Every once in a while it woke me up. I got up and tried to kill it but as soon as I put the light on it disappeared. I hope it wore itself out last nite. Then maybe I'll get some sleep.

Goodnite dear.

I love you.

Lois

P.S. Auf Wiedersehn means "until we meet again".

I scoured the August, 1952 editions of the Toronto Star newspaper to try to find an article that matched the incident to which my Mom referred in that letter.

My grandparents were in Syracuse from August 13 – 18 that year. Since Mom wrote the letter on Aug. 25, the article could have appeared any time between Aug. 13 and Aug. 25. The Toronto Star printed a lot of sensational stories from just across the border, and small, amusing stories from as far away as Kansas. With her next letter, she enclosed an entire page from that newspaper dated Aug. 20, 1952. One side was devoted to an Agnew Surpass shoe store ad. On the other side was a continuation of a front-page story about three boys who spent eighteen hours clinging to the debris of their shattered boats following an accident on Lake Simcoe before being rescued dramatically by float plane the next day. I figured maybe the story had appeared in that Aug. 20th edition of the paper and she'd sent Dad the wrong page, so I went over that particular day's paper several times. Nothing.

Finally, I found it in the Aug. 23, 1952 edition. **"Children Print Sign Defeat Speed Cops"** *read the little headline. The article was small. It read:*

> "The busy thoroughfare looked like speeders' territory. The police set up their electric timer and rat and waited. Lots of cars passed - all moving sedately within the limit. Patrolman Nicholas Margianno gunned his motorcycle and sped around the block. His catch: Two youngsters with

a sign reading: "Danger. Slow down. Police ahead."

*****

Having a Crosley television was a pretty cool thing in 1952. (Image copyright Shari Blaney/Alamy.)

We had a black and white television when I was a kid. One day, my great-uncle down the street got a colour one. Word got around fast. I brought my friends, and my great-aunt, Nana's sister, let us creep down the basement stairs and quietly watch it from behind him where he sat in air-conditioned comfort (also a luxury in 1970) in his armchair, puffing on a cigar, watching golf, mostly. Their bug-eyed, sinus-challenged Pekingese dog, Ching, snorted and snuffled behind us. We were bored by the golf, freaked out by Ching, but mesmerized by the colour on the screen.

Didn't Have Room

Hello Dear,

Didn't have room in the other letter for clipping – so am putting it in here.

Love

Lois

(Inside this envelope was the folded page of the Aug. 20 Toronto Star with the Agnew Surpass shoe store ad on one side and the story about the near-drownings on Lake Simcoe on the other. Postage was 4 cents at the time, but, like today, the envelope could only weigh so much before extra postage was charged.)

Playing Records and Smoking

Dear Bill,

Received your letters yesterday, but thought you were going to phone last nite so I didn't answer them right away. I'm sorry I wasn't home on Sun. when you called. Glad you did call anyway. I was a little worried. Thought you would let me know you got back ok, but I didn't get any mail until Mon. I guess you were too busy to write me until Fri.

Last nite Mom, Barby, & I went to the show. We went right after work so we could get home before 10:00 PM in case you phoned. Went to Shea's & saw *Where's Charley?* – a musical comedy. It was originally a stage play starring Ray Bolger. When they made a movie of it they didn't substitute any of the actors. Used the same ones who played on the stage. It was really funny! I wish you could have seen it. You would have enjoyed it.

I'm 6 – 12 today & am off both Wed. & Thur. Nice, eh? Am sitting on my bed playing records, smoking & of course writing this letter. Mom & Dad are redecorating the house. They have done the 2 bedrooms & are working on the dinette now. The house simply reeks of paint.

They painted three walls of their room in red shade. It's supposed to be raspberry, but it looks like maroon. The ceiling is pale green. The wall that their bed is against is done in wallpaper. It has red flowers on it. The same colour red as their walls and a pale green background exactly the same colour as the ceiling. The woodwork is all pale green. It looks real smart. Before I tell you about our room I want to tell you I had absolutely nothing to do with the choice of colour scheme. It was Barby's idea. We figured since it wouldn't be my room for very much longer that she should have it done in whatever way she pleased. So – it is done in sunshine yellow and a guardsman brown at least that's what <u>they</u> call it. It looks more like s--- to me. I didn't say anything though. I said it looks nice. Besides, it's what she wanted! She has to live with it longer than I do. The ceiling & wall which our cupboards are on are done in yellow. The rest of the walls are brown. The woodwork & window frames are yellow. We didn't paint any doors of course. They were all left in the natural wood. The dinette & living room will be dark green & ceilings very pale green. The back wall of the dinette will be papered. It has a cream background and a goldish coloured stripe. It is also real smart. Wouldn't you know the only room I don't like has to be my own?

Well, I suppose you've heard & read all about our big jailbreak here in Toro. Barby & I were on our way to work about 8:00, an hour after they discovered they were gone. We were on a King car & traffic on Broadview was lined up from Withrow on. We couldn't figure out what was holding it up because we didn't even know about the break. Then one of the ladies on the streetcar told us about it. We finally moved down the street until we were right in front of the jail. You should have seen it. There were policemen all over the place. Police cruisers were parked all over the street. Reporters were taking pictures. It was quite a sight. Let me know if you read the papers. If not, I'll send them to you.

Other than that, nothing exciting has happened here since you left. I do miss you dear – very much. Seeing you again has made me miss you more. I wish you would come back to Toronto. It's an awful feeling to know that all you'll ever want is 400 miles away from you. I may come up for Nov. 1st & 2nd. The 1st & 2nd are a Sat. & Sun. I should also have Fri. the 31st Oct. off & am going to request Mon. Nov. 3rd. Do you think you will have my ring by then? I'm coming up any way.

Well dear, it's noon now, so I suppose I'd better get dressed & have something to eat.

All my love

Lois

Mom's streetcar was slowed down by one of the most celebrated jailbreaks in Toronto history. The Boyd gang, based in Toronto, was a notorious and inventive crew of bank robbers and jail breakers. One of the gang members had an artificial limb, and managed to conceal a hacksaw blade which they used to saw through the prison bars. Edwin Alonzo Boyd was the leader of the gang, and the most famous. He had been in trouble with the law since his teenage years, and would sometimes attract crowds of young female admirers when being escorted by police to and from courthouses or jails. That bad boy appeal . . . he moved to British Columbia after serving time for the robberies and escape in 1952 and lived under an assumed name until he died in his eighties.

After the particular jail break that delayed Mom, the fugitives fled up the Don River Valley to North York.

Susan Goldbenberg wrote in a history column for the North York Mirror:

> "While police and reporters swarmed the jail yard, assuming that the escapees were hiding on the roof, the fugitives slowly made their way through the nearby Don River ravines up north. At that time the area was largely bush, broken only by the river and railway tracks.
>
> A mile north of Leslie and Sheppard they found an abandoned barn far back from the road and moved in. The CNR ran through

the property; Boyd thought they could hop on a freight train and go west.

The gang thought they were safe – so certain that one member, Willie Jackson, went to Sheppard and Yonge to buy food and cigarettes. For fruit they picked apples from nearby trees. They spent their time going for strolls, believing they would be regarded as tramps. However, several North Yorkers in the area recognized them and called the police."

From left, Norman Boyd, Edwin Alonzo Boyd and William Jackson pictured escorted by police in Oct. 1952. - Toronto Star Archives. Used with permission.

All the men were captured at the barn in North York on September 16, 1952. Steve Suchan and Lennie Jackson, who had murdered policeman Edmund Tong several months earlier, were executed by hanging at the Don Jail on December 16 that same year. Edwin Boyd and William Jackson received long prison sentences, although both were paroled in the 1960's. It's not clear why Edwin's brother, Norman, is in the photo. He wasn't one of the bank robbers. One source suggests he was allowing Edwin to hide in a rented apartment prior to the arrest that landed Edwin in the Don Jail before the infamous break-out.

The Don Jail would be the site of the last execution in Canada ten years after Suchan and Jackson's hanging. The double hanging of murderers Arthur Lucas and Ronald Turpin took place there on December 11, 1962.

****

Shea's Hippodrome was only five years away from demolition when Mom and her sister went there to see "Where's Charley?" Nathan Phillips Square now dominates the spot where it used to stand before it was torn down to make room for Toronto's new city hall. When Shea's opened in 1914, it was one of the largest movie palaces and theatres of its kind in the world. Its famous Wurlitzer organ now resides in Toronto's Casa Loma.

Shea's Hippodrome, interior and exterior, 1914.
Images courtesy of City of Toronto Archives.

****

"Where's Charley?" was a 1952 British musical comedy that starred Ray Bolger, most famous for playing The Scarecrow in The Wizard of Oz. The laughs center around Bolger disguising himself as his own aunt so that a gathering involving some young women can

be properly chaperoned. However, turns out the gals brought their own chaperone, a man who falls for Charley's "aunt". Drag performances never seem to go out of style. For my generation, it was Tootsie, and for the next, Mrs. Doubtfire.

*****

Mom's critique of her sister's colour choices stem from her penchant for interior decorating. Had she been born into a generation or a family that supported women having their own pursuits beyond marriage and child-rearing, she might have considered a career in that field. She never tired of imagining new décor for rooms in our family home, and was always excited to realize her visions.

After Mom and Dad downsized to a condo, she exercised full control over interior furnishings, colour schemes, and layout, as much as she could, anyway. Dad, once settled into his comfort zone, didn't like change. So, several things my Mom wanted to do during the years they lived there were just tucked away into the back of her mind. After Dad died in June of 2020, Mom plunged into a frenzy of making all the changes she'd wanted to make for years. She was so enthusiastic and impatient to get going on all these projects that my sister and I dubbed her "manic mama". I think keeping busy was a strategy for pushing away her grief. However, she had an amazing eye for what would look good in a particular space. And she was always right. It's clear from this letter that even from a young age, she paid close attention to decorating details.

I'm Bored Stiff!

Sept. 11/52

Dear Bill,

There isn't much I can say in this letter. I wrote you last nite & nothing much has happened since then & now. Today is my day off again. I'm at a loss for something to do. Am fed up with staying in. Lately, I've been going out with Mom & Barby quite a bit, but I don't really enjoy myself. Mostly we go to shows. I see all the fellows & girls sitting there together & I start wishing you were beside me holding my hand. To tell the truth I'm bored stiff! But like you always say, dear – I guess I'll survive.

Was glad to hear your cold is clearing up. Is Lillie feeling any better? I'm going to send her a card. What's the matter with her anyway?

How did you make out with the Genl. Mgr.? I was hoping you would like him but apparently you don't.

Diane is supposed to call today but so far I haven't heard from her. She came to Toro with her Dad to buy a new coat. He knows some people in the wholesale business so she can get it a lot cheaper thru them. Hope she calls soon. Then I'll have something to do for the rest of the day.

This is my last sheet of writing paper. I guess I better buy some more when I go out to mail this letter.

Dad just came home. He is teaching at the plant school again. Classes haven't started yet so he has some spare time on his hands. They are still painting the living room. He'll most likely finish it this pm. While he paints, Mom & I usually take the car & do some shopping. Nice, eh?

Lunch is just about ready so I'll go now dear.

All my love

Lois

P.S. Don't forget to write your Mom.

Dad's relationship with his Mom and the rest of his family was fraught. I rarely heard anything about the relatives on his side unless the comment was negative. We only visited a couple of times a year, to my grandparents' house on Charles Street in Port Hope, ON. "God knows why they ever moved out there," said my Dad once. As it turned out, both sides of his family had ties to that more easterly geography.

His father, Percy, was born in Uxbridge, where his father worked as an iron moulder. The family moved to Toronto to be closer to the Toronto Hospital for Sick Children because at the age of six, Percy needed surgery on his leg. The story has it that his mother took a tumble down some stairs with him in her arms as an infant, and his leg was damaged in the fall.

Dad's mother, Maude, was raised in Brockville where her father worked all his life as a carpenter. She went to live with her older, married sister in Toronto when she was about ten years old. Not that my father told me any of that. It's possible he didn't know it himself. Discovering the family history on that side took years of research.

Along with my mother's letters, my father kept two letters his mother wrote to him. Both are short. And both hint at the caustic style of communication for which she was famous.

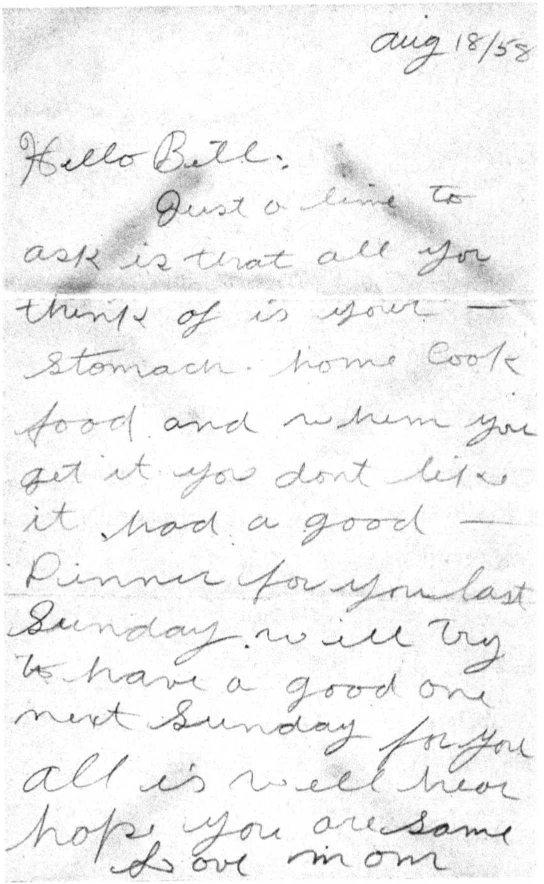

One of the letters from Nana Long. The letter appears
to have a date of 1958 on it, but it was in an envelope
postmarked 1953. Transcription below.

*Hello, Bill. Just a line to ask is that all you think of is your
stomach. Home cook food and when you get it you don't
like it. Had a good Dinner for you last Sunday. Will try
to have a good one next Sunday for you. All is well hear
(sic). Hope you are same. Love Mom.*

You Wouldn't Be Saving Any Money

Sept. 10/52

Dear Bill,

I was worried when I read that you caught cold. Take good care of yourself honey. If it doesn't clear up soon see a doctor! I thought you might catch a cold after your visit to Toro but I didn't expect it to be a real bad one.

The weather here has been cool since you left. Cool that is, until yesterday. All of a sudden it warmed up again. Today was real hot & sticky. It's still very warm out. I'm writing this letter from the coolest spot in the house – the recreation room.

Mom & I went to the show tonite. We went to see *High Noon.* It's still playing at the Odeon Danforth. We met Don & Jean there. I was down at Jean's this p.m. & she told me they were going so I said maybe we would see them there & sure enough we did.

Diane wrote to say she would be in Toro tomorrow. I don't have to work so we'll be able to see each other I imagine she'll want to go over to the school for a while to visit some of the kids.

I'm going to go to the night school at E.Y.C. this year. Will be taking typing & shorthand. Classes are Mon. & Thurs. I think the Bell will guarantee one day work on Mondays. That's the night they teach the new lessons. Then on Thurs. they practice them. Of course, I'll try to get day work on Thurs. As much as possible but as long as I can attend Monday's classes it will be ok. Barby is also taking the course so if I do miss anything she'll be able to show me. It starts in Oct. & ends before Easter. It costs $10.00. I think it's well worth it, don't you?

In your letter you said you might ask for a transfer to Hamilton. I don't think it would be a wise move. It would probably cost you more to live there & you couldn't save any money. I think the best thing to do is to find out for sure if you're going to get that selling job in Toro. If so, you might just as well stay where you are until then. After all, if you did get a transfer you would be making the same amount of money. You would be closer to Toro., therefore you would come to see me more often. It would cost you a lot of money to travel back & forth. It all adds up to one thing. You wouldn't be saving any money whatsoever and until we do save some we can't get married & I want to be married to you more than anything in the world, dear. So you think everything over carefully & let me know what you decide.

It's getting late so I better close now. I'm going to mail this letter & then get ready for bed. Please take good care of that cold. I love you dear.

Lois

High Noon was an American western starring Gary Cooper. It was nominated for seven academy awards (and won four of them, including a best actor Oscar for Cooper) and was in the top ten highest grossing U.S. films of that year.

****

Mom attended East York Collegiate Institute until about grade 11, when she quit to work at the Bell. I attended the same high school in the late 70's and early 80's and wanted to quit long before graduation, but the days of getting an instant full-time job with decent pay at the age of sixteen were over. I stuck it out. The entire four years I attended that school, the words "Smoke Gold" were spray painted on the wall near the entrance doors on Coxwell Avenue. It seemed like good advice at the time.

Boy, Was It Hot!

Sept. 14/52

Dear Bill,

Just finished eating breakfast. I slept in this morning. It's my day off. Worked 5 – 11 last nite & boy was it hot! The temperature was about 90. It's a lot cooler today though & it looks like rain. I'm sorry I forgot to send you my time last week. This week I'm 8 – 5 Mon., Tues., Wed., Thurs., & Fri. I'm getting my P.B.X. training. Have Sat. & Sun. off Sat. is the day of the Buffalo trip. The weekend of the 27th we may be going to North Bay. We're going to try to leave Fri. Nite & go back Sun. nite.

Fri. I was broken 10 so I went to the show & saw *The Merry Widow.* It was very good. I still haven't picked up that money from Agnew's. Was supposed to get it last Sat., but forgot. Was going to get it Fri., but went to the show instead. I guess I'll go up this coming Fri. nite.

Has your cold gone away yet? How is Lillie? I sent her a card on Thurs. Diane came over to see me Thurs. nite, but she didn't stay very long because they had to leave early to go back to Sarnia. One of her boyfriends drove them down & back.

Would you make very much extra money if you drove a taxi on Sundays? You might get all tired out doing that, you know, because it means you'll be working 7 days a week. You need some time for relaxation. I suppose if you went to bed early during the week it wouldn't be too bad.

I can hardly wait until I go up there in Nov. I'll be so happy to see you again honey. I miss you very much.

Well dear, I'll have to close now. I'm not dressed yet & I have to clean up this bedroom. Goodbye for now.

All my love

Lois X

Seems it was okay for my Mom to forget to do stuff, but woe betide Dad if he was slow to act on any mission she assigned him!

****

Mom sure went to a lot of movies! "The Merry Widow", starring Lana Turner and Fernando Lamas was another musical/romance/comedy in which a count from a small, fictional, nearly bankrupt European country pursues a wealthy American widow in the hopes that her fortune will save the kingdom.

****

After purchasing the land on Callander Bay just outside of the city of North Bay, Uncle Bill and Aunt Eva built their own house further up from the cottages on what everyone called "the point". Eventually, my Mom's parents bought a parcel partway between the point and the cottages, and in 1961, her Dad, my Grandpa Ed, built a seasonal home where they intended to spend the summers of their retirement. It wasn't to be. He died unexpectedly from cancer in 1966. My grandmother kept the place for several years, but it was sold around 1975. We'd go up every summer, and my sister and I would play on the rocks near the shore for hours. One of my earliest memories is waking in the sun porch of the cottage at dawn to the sound of a fishing boat headed out on the glassy bay.

I'm Disgusted

A MAN returned to his office one Monday morning showing signs of a very strenuous week-end. One of his good friends found him hunched over his desk with his head buried in his arms.

"What in heaven's name have you been doing?" asked the friend.

"Fishing through the ice," groaned the sufferer.

"Fishing through the ice! For what?"

"Cherries," was the answer.

— *The Wall Street Journal*

Sept. 16/15 (sic)

Dear Bill,

Enclosed please find a joke cut out of Reader's Digest. I think it's funny. Don't you? Nobody else does. I'm disgusted.

This will have to be a short letter, honey. I have to get up at 6 tomorrow. Think I'm going to like working on the P.B.X. It's very interesting.

The police caught Boyd Suchan & the 2 Jacksons. Goodness knows how long they'll keep them this time before they make another break. Did you read about them in the papers?

Mom just made some coffee. Will be back in about 15 minutes, Dear.

Well, I stretched those 15 minutes into 25. I also ate a hot dog. It had onion on it. You sure wouldn't want to hug me now – my breath would knock you over. Now to top it off, I'm going to have a cigarette – an American one at that.

Was happy to hear from you Sun. I thought perhaps you had given up trying to reach me. Whenever you phone I can never think of anything to say – but after I hang up I can think of a million & one things I wanted to ask you.

It looks like we won't be able to go to North Bay the weekend we planned. Barby wants to see some girl from work get married & the wedding is Sat. 27th Sept. I don't know if we'll plan to go later or not. Will let you know about it anyway.

Am going to bed now, dear. I love you.

Lois

P.S. I think I might be able to manage a baby boy for you – but not right now. Will later do?

You can imagine the reaction my sister and I had when we read <u>that</u> line!

They barely managed any kids at all. They were ten years into the marriage before they had me, another two before they had my sister, and that was it. Although smoking featured a fair bit in their early lives together, I never saw either one of them with a cigarette. I was actually pretty surprised to find out that they both had been regular smokers.

*****

In the 1950's, Bell Telephone operators used cord circuits, manually switching calls to manage company switchboards. PBX stood for Private Branch Exchange, and the way my Mom is using the term, it referred to electronic switching systems that were replacing the manual systems.

*****

As noted previously, Suchan and Lennie Jackson never did get a chance to make another jail break. Their crime spree ended with that capture and subsequent hanging.

Thought You Hated Kids

Sept. 18/52

Dear Bill,

Read your nice long letter when I came home tonite. I showed Mom the diagrams of the store & did she ever get a kick out of them! I don't know why but she thought they were real funny. I also showed her the poem. We both laughed at that. Where did Lillie find it?

It poured rain all last night & most of today. Everything went wrong today & I was real tired when I got home. Went over to Simpsons after work to buy a blouse. Didn't get it though. I bought a white wool suit. It's not a pure white – kind of creamy. It's a perfect fit. Can't you just picture me juggling that suitbox in the 5 o'clock rush? It was grim, believe me.

Was surprised to hear about your bowling. You didn't seem to care much about it when you were in Toro. What does O.N.R. stand for? Was also surprised to hear about your job at the church. Thought you hated kids. But if it keeps you away from other women I'm all for it. Hope you enjoy it.

Have you decided to take that job driving the taxi? Did you find out anything more about the selling job in Toro? I hope you get it. I'm tired of being so far away from you. There's absolutely nothing for me to do except wait for my mail & answer it. I'm sick of going out with girls all the time. It's so lonely without you honey. Sometimes I sit and play nearly all our records. I've played *I'll Never Be Free* so much that it's all scratchy sounding. I'm sorry we won't be able to make it to North Bay. I was hoping we might get to see each other again before Nov. I can hardly wait to get my ring. I'll feel so much better after I get it, dear.

Tomorrow I am going to the business office to watch a Service Representative at work. It is considered part of the P.B.X. training. I'll spend all morning with her so the day should go fairly fast. We leave at 8 Sat. morning for our Buffalo Trip. Will be seeing Sophie Tucker at the Town casino. Goodness knows what time we'll get back home. The girls who have been before say it is usually about 3:00 Sun. morn. I'll have to take a taxi home from the bus terminal.

Am going to bed now honey. I love you very much.

Lois

Dad hated kids?!!! Well, not his own, I guess. He was a good Dad.

O.N.R. stood for Ontario Northland Railway.

Mom was certainly obsessed with that ring. Maybe she felt like the engagement wasn't real until she had it, felt she couldn't really say, "I'm engaged!" without a rock on her finger to show people. Maybe she worried Dad would change his mind. It's clear that she didn't want any pretty Kirkland Lake girls turning his head.

*****

"I'll Never Be Free", sung by Tennessee Ernie Ford and Kay Starr, reached Number 2 on the U.S. country chart in 1950. My Mom's musical tastes always leaned a bit towards country. She embraced The Eagles when they came along in the 70's. "Take It To The Limit" became her favourite song.

There was a vinyl record album in my parents' collection that featured a blonde woman on the front with a microphone and was titled: Sophie Tucker – Last of the Red Hot Mamas. I picked it up one day when I was about five years old, and got ready to put it on the record player, but my grandmother saw what I was about to do and jumped in. "Oh no," she said. "Not that one. That one's dirty!" I looked at it. It looked as clean as any of the other record albums. She took it out of my hands and gave me Herb Alpert and the Tijuana Brass to put on instead. So, I ended up with a taste for live trumpets instead of vaudeville jazz and early feminist humour. By today's standards, Sophie Tucker was tame, but a lot of her material was risqué for the time. She was pretty famous, and seeing her live at the Town Casino would have been amazing.

I'll Try To Draw a Picture

Sept. 21/52

Dear Bill,

I read your letter this AM about 2:30. That's the time I got home from Buffalo. We had a terrific time. Arrived there about 12 noon. Our reservations at the casino were for 6:30 PM so we had the whole afternoon to ourselves. Most of the girls (there were 35) went shopping. Five of us went together & did we ever have fun! I bought a black velvet evening blouse. It has cap sleeves & there is a zipper on the left side. It starts at the bottom of the blouse and goes right up under the arm. There's a deep V in the front & back & it is almost off the shoulder. I'll try to draw a picture of it for you.

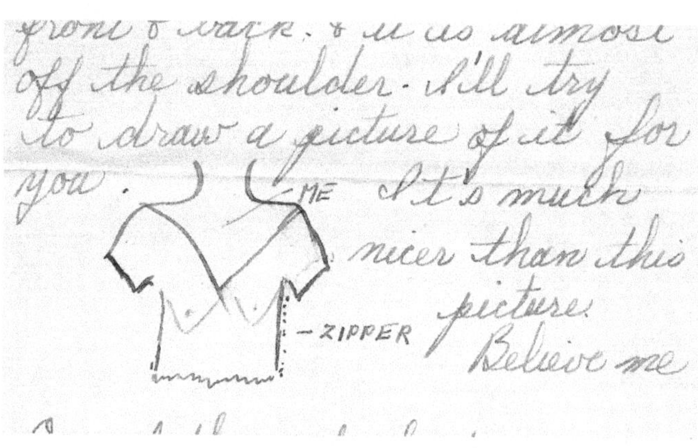

It's much nicer than this picture. Believe me.

One of the girls had on a suit & she didn't wear a blouse underneath the jacket so she wore it back over the border for me. Also bought 2 pr earrings, 1 pr for Barby the other pr for me. Oh yes & a couple of fancy hankies & I stole a hand towel from the Hotel Statler. Sophie Tucker wasn't playing at the Casino after all. They changed the bill. Instead there was a Negro piano player named Maurice Rocco. He played jazz & boy was he good!! I wish you could have heard him. The Casino is really nice inside. It's very large & has a high ceiling done in that deep blue mirror glass. They served us drinks & I had quite a few. Mostly gin. After the dinner & show at the Casino we went to one of those stores that sell those real small bottles of wines & such. We bought some small bottles of cognac for souvenirs, but we drank it on the way home so all I have left is the empty bottle. One thing I didn't buy was American cigarettes. I don't like them.

I almost forgot to tell you, we had our picture taken in the Casino. The girl came & took one of us sitting at the table. There are seven of us in it. They put the picture in a folder for you. I bought one. It is an exceptionally good one of me, at least that's what everyone says. It's too big for me to send up in a letter so you'll have to wait until I come up again before you see it. Well, that's enough about Buffalo. The rest you'll have to wait for me to tell you in Nov. You know what I mean – the dirty songs & jokes I heard on the bus. We sat in the back seat both ways.

How did your bowling go last Wednesday? Did you manage to stay sober? I hope so. It's too bad you couldn't keep up the insurance. You should really have some kind you know. Am glad you didn't take that driving job Sundays. I didn't really want you to, you know. What did you mean when you wrote, "It was mean of Diane"? I don't understand.

I suppose I did get bored once in a while when you were in Toro., dear, but it wasn't the same feeling I have now. Anyway, that feeling didn't last long. The one I talk about is with me most of the time. I guess you just don't understand what I mean.

I do like my new nickname. Right now if I could hear your voice – even if you swore at me – I'd love it. I must have it real bad honey. I've never felt this way about anybody before. I just plain love you dear and the more you're away from me the worse I get. If I write any more I'm going to cry, so goodnite dear.

All my love

Lois

Well, Mom wasn't an artist. Those pointy breasts with nipple dots were drawn in pencil whereas the rest of the drawing was in ink. I'm wondering if Dad drew those in after he got her letter. We'd love to know what the nickname was. My Dad sometimes called her "Gabby" and maybe that was when it started. Mom did like to talk. It's hard to imagine she was tongue-tied on the telephone.

*****

Casinos continued to be a big draw for Mom and Dad. Almost all their vacations involved at least one. In their final years together, they enjoyed going to Seneca in New York, possibly because it was a relatively short drive. They didn't like flying much. Although Mom was thin as a young woman, she put on weight later, and found airplane seats cramped and uncomfortable.

*****

Mom nags Dad about drinking a few times, but it doesn't sound like she was holding back much herself on the New York trip.

Maurice Rocco was a famous American piano player in the forties and fifties, known for playing standing up, no piano stool. His energetic nightclub performances made him a star, and he toured Europe and southeast Asia before settling permanently in Thailand, where he was murdered at the age of 60. So, while they didn't get to see Sophie Tucker, they certainly saw a pretty good act!

I Love You So Much

Sept. 22/52

Dear Bill,

Just finished washing up the dishes. Thought I would answer your letter before I make the beds. Mom has been working at Laura Secords these last 2 weeks. They are very short of staff so she's helping them out. That means she doesn't get much done in the AM before she goes, so we all pitch in & do it at nite.

Dad has finished decorating upstairs. Now he is laying tile in the cellar. Has the laundry room almost finished. The tile is supposed to be Pomeranian Red but looks just brown to me. On Sun. our hot water tank sprung a leak. All the cellar floor around the oil burner was flooded. Boy! What a mess! Dad carried out 12 pailfuls of water. He fixed it up, but if it leaks again we'll have to buy a new one.

My suit is much different from my grey one although it fits me just as well. I think you know the kind of suit I mean. It's that knitted wool. We used to see quite a few of them in the store windows along the Danforth. I haven't seen one exactly the same as mine yet. I'm glad I got one that's different because quite a few of the girls have them. The skirt is straight – no flare in it whatsoever. There is no zipper in the skirt. The waistband is made of elasticized wool – stretches to fit your waist. The top is plain, it fits down over the waist & ends just above the hips. It has a Peter Pan collar & a zipper in the back at the neck. A belt with a gold buckle fits around the waist of the top. It's hard to explain. That's the best I can do.

My time for this wk. is Wed. 9:30 – 1:30 5:30 – 8:30. Thurs. 12 – 8. Fri. 8:30 – 5:30, Sat. OFF, Sun. OFF. No use telling you my time for Mon. & Tues. You won't have this letter until Wed. or Thurs. Happy Anniversary dear. I hope this letter reaches you Wed. If not, Happy Anniversary anyway. Two years & five months is a long time. Every bit of it has gone fast except this last month & a half. They've just crawled by because you haven't been with me. I know they'll keep right on crawling until we're together again.

I'm real pleased that Mr. Shaw liked you. I'm hoping with all my heart that you'll be back to stay at Xmas time, so darling, do your very best. I love you so much.

Lois X

Mom made it sound like Nana was doing the local Laura Secord store a favour. My Aunt Barbara informed me that the real reason Nana was working that summer was to save up enough money for a bus trip to California to visit her eldest child, my Aunt Irene. Regular folk didn't fly in the 1950's. People took trains or buses where they wanted to go. It was still common to get passage on a ship if travelling across the ocean.

Laura Secord products featured prominently in my childhood. I associate their oblong lollipops wrapped in clear cellophane with Nana, the cottage, and special occasions. I would hold the tightly wound paper stick in my mouth long after the candy was gone until it was wet enough to pick one edge loose and start unwinding. The only reward was a curled sheet of paper, but it never failed to fascinate me that a flimsy piece of paper could be made into something so rigid. My Dad pointed out to me that paper came from trees. That made sense.

*****

Here is "Happy Anniversary" again, always around the same time each month. This letter referring to the anniversary of love gives us a date, though. If it was two years and five months on Sept. 22, 1952, that put their commitment to one another on April 22, 1950, when they were 15 and 17 respectively. In that case, it's not surprising that she "never felt this way about anybody before". How many potential lifelong love interests does one have before the age of 15?

*****

Shopping on the Danforth was the thing to do in the 50's, much as shopping on King Street had been the thing to do in the earlier part of the century. After the Prince Edward Viaduct was built across the ravine in 1918, Danforth Avenue began to see more commercial development. By the 1930's it was well on the way to becoming a shopping district for everything from used cars to fashions, and in the 1950's you could stroll for blocks, especially around Mom and Dad's old Riverdale neighbourhood, and window shop or grab lunch at any number of cafés or diners. With the exception of a quick grocery run, women used to dress up to go shopping. It was a major outing. No one would have dreamed of going into a department store in pyjama bottoms in 1952.

Have You Written Your Mom Yet?

Sept. 24/52

Dear Bill,

Received your letter today & I've got news for you, boy, it's only 2 years & 5 months. You miscounted. Never mind, the thought was there & that's the only thing that matters to me. I wish I had known about your Mom's anniversary sooner. I would have sent a card. I don't expect to be up before Nov. I'll get the needles for Lillie's machine. Does she need them very bad? If so I can send them up.

If you're going to go hunting this fall, go bear hunting. I'd just love a bearskin rug. You're so far north you might even shoot me a nice white polar bear. I'm only kidding you dear. Please be careful when you go hunting. You know a lot of serious accidents can happen.

Have you started your craft class at the church yet? I'm curious to see how it works out. Is Joyce still planning on going to the Bell? Let me know how the new girl makes out. Is she nice looking? (meow)

My time for next wk is Mon. 8 – 5, Tues. 8 – 5, Wed. OFF, Thurs, 1 – 9, Fri. 5 – 11, Sat. 8 – 5, Sun. OFF.

Thurs. I am loaned to the Grover office. That's at Main & Kingston Rd. I don't think I'll like it, but there's nothing I can do about it. Mon. I start nite school. Am really looking forward to it.

Am very tired tonite. I have a pain in the back of my neck. It's been bothering me 2 days now. I must have been sitting in a draught or something. Anyway, I'm going to take a 222 before I got to bed. That may help to relax me.

I won't let the Boultons know where you are if they should happen to phone here. Have you written your Mom yet? You told her you would, you know.

Well sweet, I'm going to bed now. I love you.

Lois

No idea who the Boultons were. We knew my Dad liked fishing when he was younger, but this was the first I'd heard of him going hunting. Neither my sister nor I can picture Dad doing crafts with kids at a church. That had to be something he was getting drawn into by his devoutly Catholic sister. Or maybe Mom was right to worry. Maybe there was a pretty girl in Kirkland Lake who liked to hang out at the church.

****

Mom seems concerned about Dad's relationship with his own mother. I'm sure it was puzzling to her, being as close to her own family as she was. And I'm equally sure that she felt it was important, if they were going to marry, for Dad's mother to like her, so not having sent an anniversary card would have bothered her. Mom was a great one for cards. She didn't miss a birthday, anniversary, you name it. After she died, we found a huge stack of new greeting cards she'd purchased in advance of any possible occasion.

There's No Harm In Asking

Sep. 25/52

Dear Bill,

I can't think of a thing to say, but I'm writing you anyway. Sometimes I can sit down & ramble a letter off & not give it a second thought. Then there are times like this when I haven't got a clue.

Was surprised to hear you were in a fight. The climate up there must be invigorating! You better be careful, though. Next time, he might not miss if he kicks at you. You wouldn't want to ruin our married life would you? (goodness, I'm getting as bad as you)

I think it's very inconsiderate of Gord to expect you to be satisfied with such a late lunch. Why don't you mention you would like an earlier lunch? There's no harm in asking. Do you think it's worth your while to come down Thanksgiving? I'll be working Mon., you know. So we wouldn't have much time together. I miss you terribly honey & I want so much to see you again. Nov. seems so far away, but I'm afraid that's the soonest we'll be able to see each other again. I hope we will be engaged before I go back home. Are you keeping up the payments on my ring? (mercenary aren't I?)

It's 11:20 PM now honey & I have to be up at 6:30 AM so I better close now. I love you.

Lois

Maybe not mercenary, but certainly relentless. It's a good thing Dad got her that ring eventually.

She would have considered that comment about their "married life" to be pretty risqué in 1952. Sounds like Dad could be a bit of a scrapper. He had a temper, for sure, although he mostly kept it in check. I can't picture him actually fighting with anyone.

You Belong To Me

Dear Bill,

When I came home from work tonite I was going to eat, wash my hair, take a bath & go to bed early. Well, I didn't do it. Barby asked me to go to a rugby game at E.Y. Stadium, so I went. E.Y. beat Scarb. The score was 7-6, but it was a lousy game. They haven't got half the team they used to have.

Joined a club at the Bell, It's a new one called the "Mabel Hubbard Club" named after Alexander Graham Bell's wife. There has been one in Montréal for quite a while, but it's something new for Toro. There are all different kinds of activities – sewing, leather craft, metal craft, bridge lessons, driving lessons, motor mechanics & many more. I put my name down for welfare work. Also put my name down to be on the welfare committee. I hope it has a lot to do with children because I like them. I can work things out ok. Will be going to school 2 nites a wk & most the club's activities are Mon. – Thurs. nites. Also will have to work nites. I didn't get drunk in Buffalo, dear, even though I had quite a few drinks. I was stone sober. Sorry I didn't buy you any cigarettes. Didn't think you like American cigarettes either. Haven't worn my new blouse yet. Haven't been any place where I could wear it. Am going to buy another strapless bra to wear under it. Who knows? Maybe I'll buy one with a zipper up the front.

I have to go to the dentist tomorrow AM for a checkup. Hope he doesn't find many cavities. Always costs so much to have them fixed.

You seem to be getting along good with your bowling. Keep it up you may win a prize or something, or do they have prizes?

Bought two records today. *I Went To Your Wedding* by Patti Paige & *You Belong to Me* by Jo Stafford. I especially like the words to the latter. Have you heard it?

It goes like this –

See the pyramids along the Nile . . .

Isn't it beautiful? I'm going to bed now, dear. Have to get up early for my dentist appointment.

I love you darling

Lois

EY Stadium would have been the East York Memorial Stadium attached to East York Collegiate Institute. It was the venue for any number of events. At the time, East York was an independent Borough, and had its own everything – civic center, school board, municipal council, library board, music bands, clubs, and sports teams.

****

Mabel Hubbard Bell should be just as well-known as her husband, Alexander Graham Bell. She was a scientist, interested in agriculture and food preservation, and an investor whose financial support was instrumental in early aviation research and prototypes. She also established the first Montessori school in Canada. The Bell Club, was, in the early 1990's, the oldest continuously running women's club in Canada. However, I can find no evidence of its existence now. Mabel Bell began it in 1891 in Baddeck, in Cape Breton, Nova Scotia. She modeled it after a similar club she'd seen formed in Washington D.C. Its purpose was to "stimulate the acquisition of general knowledge and to promote sociability".

In a time when the life of a married woman often meant a lack of intellectual or social stimulation outside of the home, the club offered much needed connection and camaraderie. Club chapters eventually spread from Cape Breton to other parts of the country, and club members were often at the heart of community initiatives such as establishing public libraries, or parent-teacher associations. They also sponsored cultural and literary events.

The surprising thing is that Mom joined this club. Mom and Dad typically did not get involved with service organizations, clubs, or any community groups. Apart from Mom serving on our elementary school Parent-Teacher Association, I'm at a loss to recall any other civic or neighbourhood involvement.

****

You really need to go online and listen to Jo Stafford perform "You Belong To Me". Mom wrote out the entire lyrics in her letter. The song remained on the U.S. charts for 24 weeks, and on the U.K charts for 19. I can't do her justice with words on a page. Speaking of pages, Patti Paige was the one of the best-selling American female artists of the 1950's. When some backup singers couldn't be found, she became the first pop artist to harmonize her own vocals on a recording, using technology that was new at the time. Her style isn't my cup of tea, but a lot of others felt differently. She sold over 100 million recordings.

I Hardly Know What To Tell You

Sept. 28/52

Dear Bill,

Just came home from a car ride. Uncle Ed came over for the weekend and so far the weather has been grand. Today especially. It was supposed to go to 85, but I don't think it is quite that hot. We drove out Markham way. We stopped at a roadside stand & bought some fruit. I'm so full of pears and grapes I feel as though my stomach will burst.

Last nite Barby & I went to the show. We saw *Son of Ali Baba* at the Uptown. On our way home we went into the bus terminal. Do you remember that dark-haired man who used to cashier in there? Well anyway, he remembers you. He asked me where you were because he hadn't seen you for so long. I told him you lived up north with the Eskimos.

By the way, I don't have to work Thanksgiving after all. Do you think it's worth it to come down? When would you have to go back? Can you afford to come? As for your coming back to stay dear, I hardly know what to tell you. If you did come back could you get a job with a future? I tried to tell you when you went, what it would be like to be so far away from each other. But I guess you have to live and learn. I know that sounds sarcastic, but it's not meant to be.

I wasn't surprised when you wrote we wouldn't be able to get married in April I would like very much to get married next Sept. or is that still too soon? We can't get married at all if you don't soon settle down and decide what you want to do. If you want to be near me, alright. Come back to Toro & try to get a job. If you can't find one to suit you, take one for the time being and go to nite school & take a course that will help you to get the kind of job you like. I don't mind waiting a little longer if it will be of some benefit to us in the future. I'm afraid that's the only solution I can offer dear. My dinner is ready, so I'll have to go now.

All my love

Lois

Mom was hiding her bitter disappointment in this letter. There's no way she was giving up on her dream of a spring wedding so calmly, not if I know my Mom. I'm sure there were tears shed and drama in the house.

*****

"Son of Ali Baba" is about as ridiculous as it sounds, but it starred Tony Curtis.

Before large chains had a virtual monopoly on cinema in every city, myriad small, independently owned cinemas abounded. The Uptown was at Yonge and Bloor in Toronto. By the time my friends and I were frequenting it in the 70's and 80's, it sported five separate screening rooms, and had the distinction of being one of Toronto's first multi-plex cinemas. It had already been renovated at least twice, once after a fire in 1960. When Mom went there in the 50's, it hadn't yet been damaged by the fire, and would have featured some beautiful interior architecture.

****

It doesn't surprise me that the cashier at the bus terminal knew my Dad. Everyone knew my Dad. After he died, so many people were saying, "Where's Bill?" It seems he made friends with variety store clerks, cashiers, bank tellers, custodians, you name it. Random people in their building would offer me condolences in the elevator. Not even Mom knew who half of them were.

Not long after his death, I was back in Thunder Bay, shopping with my mask on at the local country market. A woman, also masked, stopped me with a bright hello, which I returned, although I wasn't sure who she was. Then she immediately asked, "How's Bill?" to which I responded that he had died. At the precise moment that I registered the shock on her face, I also remembered that I wasn't in Toronto and that there was no way this woman could know my Dad. As she stood staring in astonishment at the news that someone she knew well had died without her knowing it, I quickly asked, "How did you know my father?"

Her face changed. "I'm sorry. I thought Bill was your husband. I'm mistaking you for someone else." We laughed awkwardly about making masked-face mistakes, and went our separate ways. I'm sure she walked away relieved.

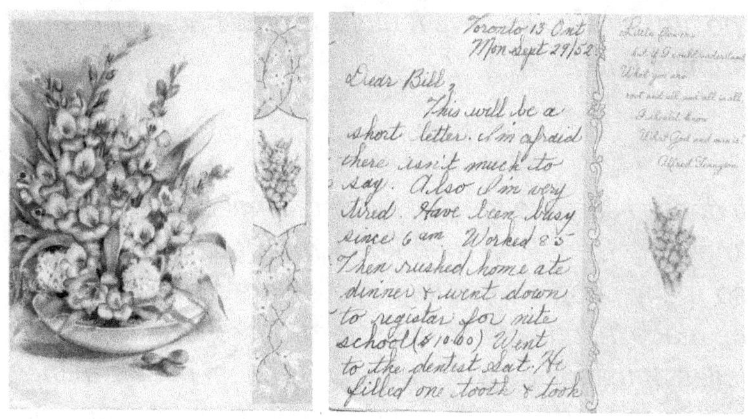

I Want You Back Here

Sept. 29/52

Dear Bill,

This will be a short letter. I'm afraid there isn't much to say. Also I'm very tired. Have been busy since 6 am. Worked 8 – 5. Then rushed home, ate dinner & went down to register for nite school ($10.00). Went to the dentist Sat. He filled one tooth & took an x-ray ($5.00). Also have 2 other cavities to be filled. My, how my money goes.

A friend of Mom's asked her if Barby & I would like to do church work. By that she means taking a class at the Sunday School. It would be Sun. mornings. I would like to teach a class – but don't know if I would be good enough. What do you think, dear?

My neck is better now. But if you had been here to massage it, I'm sure it would have been cured much quicker. (or would it?) (ha ha) You <u>are</u> awful. No, my "you know what" has <u>not</u> come – yet. But don't worry. I'm not. (not much I'm not!)

I hope that new girl doesn't get any ideas about you <u>or</u> vice versa. I can't help it, dear. I guess I'm just the very jealous type. But for all I say – I do trust you & always will until I have very good reason not to. I miss you very much & if I were free to do so I'd hop the first train up there & drag you back to Toro.

I only wish you could find a job that suited you down here. Then we could be near each other again. I try to tell myself that it's for both our good that you're up there, but I guess I'm not very convincing because I always end up with the same thought. I want you back here! I love you very much.

Goodnite darling

Lois

Of course, Mom's referring to her period. And if Dad was asking her about it, there could only be one reason. I'm certain they would have been keeping the extent of their relationship very secret.

Although Dad's mom was already pregnant with my Aunt Rose when she married at the age of fifteen, and despite evidence suggesting that Mom's grandmother came over from England with a bun already in the oven and no marriage certificate, Mom's parents definitely would not have approved. My grandfather, in particular, came from a deeply religious background. Mom was only seventeen, and living at home, so she'd be expected to adhere to whatever her parents thought was decent behavior. Going all the way with her boyfriend before the wedding would not have fit within expectations.

****

The talk of church work was surprising to us. I guess we knew that Mom and Dad had both been taken to church as kids, or at least Sunday school in my Mom's case. She doesn't recall being taken to many services. Dad told me he was dragged to the Catholic church by his Mom, and the Presbyterian church by his father, sometimes on the same day! But by the time we were old enough to ask questions about religion and God, both of them were pretty firm atheists. My Mom said she had grown tired of asking questions and always being told, "It's a mystery." And my Dad simply had no use for any of it. In his eyes, religious belief was a sign of an inferior mind, superstitious nonsense. That being said, he had respect for individuals. I do remember vividly one incident on our street when we were kids. The United church minister and his family lived several doors down from us. Across the road from them lived a hot-tempered Frenchman with a troubled teenaged kid. The kid did something that caused Frank, the minister, to go out on the street and speak to the neighbour. The neighbour lost his temper and started swearing. My Dad frowned and said, "You don't talk to a minister that way," put down his rake, and went over to mediate and calm things down. But the idea that either one of them would volunteer to do crafts with kids at a church or teach Sunday school conflicts with my image of them as being pretty anti-church.

*****

Dental work then, like dental work now, could really hurt the budget. $5.00 was a fair chunk of money in 1952, probably close to half a day's wages.

*****

Most of the letters were addressed to Neill's Shoe Store in Kirkland Lake, but a few at the beginning and this next one at the end were addressed care of my Aunt Lilly in Chaput Hughes, which is just outside the town of Kirkland Lake, only a few minutes driving along the highway. Everyone in my family pronounces it Chappy Hyooz *or just* Chappy. *My cousins still live there.*

*****

You can see by the postmarks that the mail was travelling quickly between Toronto and Chaput Hughes. Mom's letter is postmarked 8:30 p.m. in Toronto on Oct. 1, and is stamped in Chaput Hughes the afternoon of Oct. 2. People seemed to be getting their four cents worth out of Canada Post.

"A Fine Way to Run a Business!"

Sept. 30/52

Dear Bill,

I'm sorry for the way I acted on the telephone dear, but by the time I reached you, my nerves were so shot it wasn't funny. I got home about 6 PM & Mom told me a telegram had come for me about 5:30, but the boy said he couldn't leave it with her & that he would have to come back later. I was anxious to find out what it was so I decided to call the office & see if they would read the message to me; Mom said the messenger's uniform had CNR on it, so I called CNR Telegraphs. I explained everything to the girl. She connected me with some man & I had to explain it to him. He went away to check. He kept me waiting about 10 min. Then he came back & said, "Oh, that's from Kirkland Lake, is it?" I said I thought so & he said, well, that would be CPR. I told him about the messenger's uniform & he said that the telegram came from a branch store that handled CN <u>&</u> CP telegraphs. So he gave me a number to call. I called & explained everything to another girl. She connected me with another man & so I had to explain it all again. He said the branch that would have handled that telegram was closed, but he would try to find the message for me. He went away & I waited and waited. I was nearly frantic. Daddy kept saying, "This is a disgrace." "Suppose something is wrong with Bill." And "They shouldn't keep you waiting so long. A fine way to run a business." If he would have kept quiet it wouldn't have been so bad. But then I started thinking maybe something <u>had</u> happened to you! Finally the man found the message & read it to me. I was so relieved I almost sat down on the floor & cried.

I do want you to come back dear. I hope you do. Mother says you may stay here for a few days until you decide where to go & what to do. Do you really want to come back? I think it was very mean of Gord to take the key back like that. Do you suppose he heard you were asking around about a ride to Toro? Well, hon, I'm going to close now. Be sure to let me know if you're coming back.

All my love

Lois

Telegrams (or wires, as they were also known) were still used frequently in the 1950's in Canada. The actual wires for sending them ran along the railway lines, and telegram services were operated by CN and CPR (each of which were affiliated with different American telegraph companies) and were considered faster and more reliable than Canada Post. They were also more expensive, and were used mainly for special occasions, or emergencies. A person sending a telegram was charged per word, and so they often contained sentence fragments that gave little heed to proper grammar. Telegrams were delivered directly to the recipient by a uniformed agent.

Because they were used for urgent messages, Mom was justified in her concerns, although in this case, it appears to have been a benign message, probably regarding quick travel plans, but we have no idea what was in that one. It didn't survive. One other telegram that my father sent my mother did surface in his belongings after he died. It's very brief, was dated two months after their wedding, and simply said, "I am sorry. Please forgive me. Meet me at one o'clock at your front door. Bill"

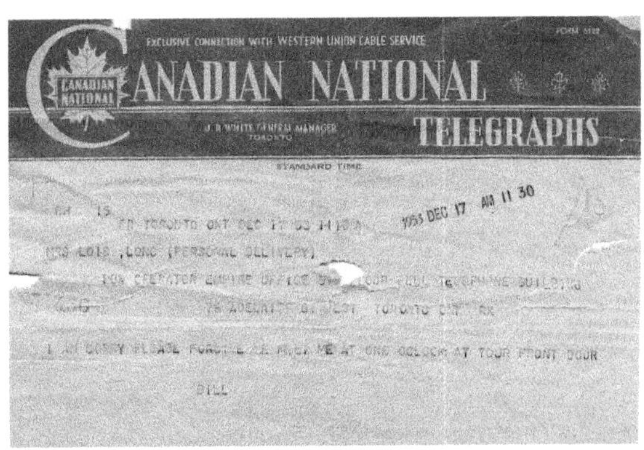

When we asked Mom about that one, she laughed and said she could not for the life of her remember what it was about. She had no memory of what he'd been so sorry for.

I was surprised to discover you can still send a telegram in Canada. The company is called Telegrams Canada, and a first-class telegram costs $18.95 plus 0.99 a word with delivery "usually within 24 hours" between major cities in Canada. For those who want to avoid leaving an email trace, I guess.

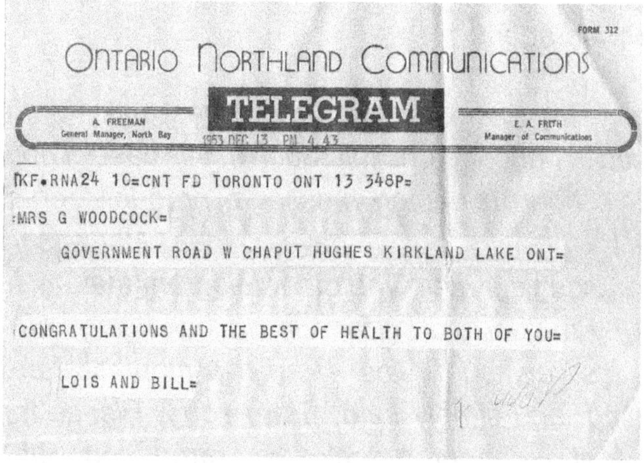

Example of a telegram my parents sent Aunt Lilly. Given the date, I'm guessing it was to congratulate her on the birth of her daughter, my cousin Judy Ann.

One Less Worry

Dear Bill,

I suppose I should have written you before this but I wasn't sure you would still be up there. I thought perhaps you might have returned this weekend. When are you coming? Mom, Dad, & I are going to North Bay Thanksgiving weekend. We're leaving Sat. AM & coming back Mon. Why don't you come back that weekend? Then you could take a train to N. Bay & we'll drive you the rest of the way. If you want to do that, write & let me know which train you'll be taking & I'll meet you at the North Bay Station. I don't care what time it gets in. I'll still meet you. Mom & Dad think it's a good idea. It certainly would save you a lot of money. Please try to come. Don't worry about having a place to stay as I told you before Mom says you can stay here until you get a chance to look around. Did you get my last letter? I sent it to Lillie's address instead of the store because I didn't know whether you would still be there. But I guess you will, for this wk anyway.

By the way "you know what" (as you call it) came, so that's one less worry. It poured rain last Wed. nite & I got caught in it. I was walking out to the store to buy some magazines & all of a sudden it just teemed. Anyway, I got drenched. Now I think I've a bit of a cold. You hurry back home. Then I can give it to you. That's all for now dear. Write soon & let me know about next weekend.

All my love

Lois

We get the feeling that our grandparents were going to be just as relieved as my Mom once Dad was back in Toronto. It couldn't have been much fun to have your teenage daughter moping around the house, lovesick and anxious all the time. We wonder if they knew, or suspected, that Lois and Bill were already sexual partners. Parents often suss out what's going on even when kids try their best to be discreet. If so, that would have made them as anxious as my Mom to see this union legitimized before a scandal erupted.

Extra Expenses

Oct. 7/52

Dear Bill,

Received two letters from you yesterday. I'm sorry I didn't write before, but as I told you, I kind of expected you home last weekend. I hope you come this weekend. It's almost impossible for me to look around for a room for you. I don't even know for sure when you'll be back. Usually people won't hold a room for you. Anyway, you know you can stay here for a few days.

Naturally I have told Mom & Dad you're coming back. They certainly don't think you're foolish. In fact, Mom has said time & time again that it's not right for us to be so far away from each other.

I worked all last weekend so this weekend I have Fri, Sat., Sun., & Mon. off Believe me, that little holiday is more than welcome. I'm 6 – 12 today broken 10 tomorrow, 8:30 – 5:30 Thurs. Isn't that awful? The only 2 nites I have off this wk. I have to go to nite school. Oh well, I asked for it.

Lately I have been reading the Sales Help wanted column. There doesn't seem to be many jobs open unless you want to travel or unless you own a late model car.

So far, I haven't saved any money for that trip up there. I was going to take it out of my next check. But I've had some extra expenses lately. My dentist bills, my fee for nite school & my books, so I haven't been able to save any money & now Christmas is coming so I'll have to save for that. I guess you haven't been able to save either.

Well, it's noon now & I'm going to make some lunch. Be sure to let me know about this weekend.

All my love

Lois

P.S. My waist is about 24". I suppose the size would be medium. What makes you think you won't see them? (ha ha yourself).

The 1952 letters end here. Presumably, Dad came back to Toronto around Thanksgiving. Maybe he even met them in North Bay. The only remaining artifact from 1952 is the birthday card Mom gave him that year. His birthday was December 14th.

PART II

The 1953 Letters

The next batch of letters we found were dated just prior to their wedding in September of 1953.

At this point, Dad is away in Montréal, taking some kind of training. We're going to assume this was industry training for the insurance company that he ended up working for, until he eventually started his own brokerage in East York in the 1970's – Long Insurance Brokers. He continued with that business until retirement. My sister worked there, and kept the business after they retired. She formed partnerships with some other small, independent brokers, and the business morphed into Generations Insurance, which is still active today on Kingston Road in Toronto.

Once again, Mom is writing him letters almost daily. They are officially engaged now. Mom has her ring, and is frantically planning their wedding.

Finally, the ring! (Photo courtesy of Beverley Wills.)

A B C D   puppies
L M N O   puppies
S A R
C M P N
G A R   puppies

A Wonderful Discovery

July 28/53

Dear Bill,

I was so glad to hear from you & finally get your address. I gather from your letter that neither you nor Al are fond of Montreal. Since you left I've been very busy & I'm really grateful because I know I would miss you twice as much otherwise. I just took your library books back on Mon. Isn't that awful? There was $1.08 due on them. It's my own fault, though, because I started to read one & kept them out until I finished.

Kay had her baby last Tues. – a girl, just what she wanted. The day she went to the hospital was my day off so I went into her place to help Mom with the kids. I was going down the cellar stairs – tripped about halfway down & made a beautiful 3 point landing at the bottom. I bruised my left elbow, took a big hunk of skin out of the right one & of course I could hardly sit down – my seat ached so much. That nite Mom, Dad, Barb & I went out to Mussleman's Lake to visit some friends. We got back to Toro about midnight & at 3:00 am I was up again, sick as a dog.

Barbara gave me a personal shower last nite & I got some lovely gifts. Mrs. Parker gave me a permanent, pleated, white nylon nightgown & Carol gave me the slip to match. Mom & Barbara gave me a set of lounging pajamas, black satin bottoms with a black & gold top & a black & gold duster housecoat to match. I got 9 pr of nylons, a cute blue leather cosmetic case & also some underwear. I was really surprised!

Dad did not make the legs for the bed. He bought us an unpainted bed to fit your mattress & spring. Wasn't it wonderful of him! We are painting them a soft tone of grey which should blend in nice with light blue. I hope it's alright with you dear. By "them" I mean the dresser & the bed. We thought it over carefully & there wasn't anything much else we could do. The finish on the dresser was definitely gone, so we could not stain & varnish it in a light wood colour. The bed could have been stained and varnished but I didn't want it one colour & the dresser another. Dad put the Masonite top on the dresser & finished the edge with wooden moulding. I bought modern looking knobs for the drawers. They look real smart. I hope you approve of my choice of colour. Please let me know.

I'm going to call Mr. Corcoran tomorrow & make arrangements to go & see him about painting the apartment.

Do you remember that camera Dad got with his suit? Well, when he got his navy suit they gave him another one & he gave it to me like he promised. I made a wonderful discovery. You don't have to hold it away from your face at all. The first one he got was broken! The one he gave me works fine. I took a film Sun. & the pictures turned out perfect. They're a good size, too. So – we now have a camera with a flash attachment!

I haven't called Al's wife yet, but am still planning to do so. I went for another fitting of my wedding dress tonite. I'm really getting excited now. Just think a little over a month & then we'll be married. It's almost too good to be true. Are you inviting Mr. Salt to the wedding? If so, what are his initials & his address? Please let me know right away because the invitations will be sent out at the end of next wk. Oh, damn! I wish you were here.

A wedding is something you plan together – not over 300 miles apart.

I guess I shouldn't have written that down but it expresses my sentiments perfectly. It's not very easy for you either honey. I know. I love you dear, always.

I feel sorry for you & Al. Sunrise Lodge sounds more like a prison than anything else, but never mind. By the time you receive this letter you will be home in 22 days & married in 36. Are you as excited as I am? I don't think anyone else could be.

I don't know my time for next week yet, but I'm 8:15 – 4:45 in the District office Mon. – Thurs. this wk. Fri. I'm 8 – 5 in my own office, off Sat. & Sun. & then I work the holiday on Mon. Will let you know next wks time as soon as possible.

I've enclosed a cute little joke – cute that is if you can understand it. All you have to do is read it thru & put the right accent in the right place.

All my love

Lois

P.S. Please be careful & don't go out on too many drinking sprees – please! - ???

Mom's joke reminds me of another that someone showed me once. It's supposed to involve an accent from a particular part of Canada. It goes like this:

MR DUCKS
MR KNOT
MR 2
CEDAR WINGS?
WHILE ALL BEEF HOOKED
MR DUCKS!

*****

The Sunrise Lodge is long gone, and appears to have left no echo of itself. A large chain hotel stands at that address now.

*****

One might expect from all the warnings and admonishments against drinking that Dad was a bit of a lush. Nothing could be further from the truth, at least, not once he had kids. I can count on one hand the number of times I remember seeing my Dad inebriated to the point where you might easily notice.

I think it was different when he was a younger man, though. He told me once that he stopped drinking at company events and parties after an uncomfortable incident when he said something he probably shouldn't have said. I can relate.

What A Disappointment!

Sept. 6/53

Dear Bill,

Received your short, short note today. Gee what a disappointment! Here I expected a nice, long letter from you. I felt so awful when you got off the streetcar on Mon. I had to swallow a big lump in my throat all the way down to work. I really hated to see you go back. It was so wonderful to have you home.

Did Al meet you ok at the bus terminal? Was the trip back very tiring? I'll bet you were whacked right out.

I went down to your Mom's place today to get your record & the credit card from the jewelers. Your Mom heard from someone (Rose, I think) that you were in Toro for the weekend. She said, "It's funny he didn't even call his parents." & I was tongue-tied, Of course, I could have given her a sarcastic remark, but I couldn't think of anything nice to say so I said nothing. Then, when I told her I wanted to get the record she said, "Bill didn't say anything to me about any records going out of the house." I was awfully embarrassed. I guess I shouldn't let things like that upset me, but I do. Also, I shouldn't complain to you about it. There's nothing you can do, but I have to tell someone & you're the only one I can tell.

I haven't gone into the jewelers yet, but I am going in tomorrow. Shall I keep the card or send it to you? (also the bill) Mom & I went out shopping today. I ordered my headdress for my wedding gown, bought a pr. of shoes & also my going away suit. My feet were so tired when we were finished, I could hardly walk. I soaked them in baking soda & hot water when we got back home. This morning I got up at 8:45, ate, dressed & then went down to your place. From there I went to Jean's & then went & met Mom at Coxwell & Danforth. We had lunch & started shopping. At 5 pm. we were finished so it's easy to understand why my feet were so tired.

Last nite, Mom & Dad & I went down to Corcoran's to discuss the painting of our apartment. The painter was there & we got everything settled. They are going to call me when they have the rooms started so I can go down & see how everything is coming along. The bedroom <u>will</u> be blue & the bathroom 2 tone yellow – very smart looking. The linoleum in the bathroom is black & white. There <u>is</u> a sink in the kitchen. It's in what once was a cupboard & there are shelves all above it for food & dishes, etc. The kitchen & living room will be done in the colours we wanted – green & gray. Our stove is a McClary 4 burner with an oven <u>and</u> a broiler. Also, there <u>is</u> a door on the kitchen. The make of refrigerator is Mayflower – an old make, but is running good. Dad saw the plug was in, but it didn't seem to be running, so he pulled the plug out at the same time blew a fuse in the back part of the house. There was a short in the wire in the plug or something. I don't understand much about it. Anyway, he fixed that & put in a new fuse for them. They were so pleased! Mrs. Corcoran said it was the only time they ever had anything fixed free. Because of his arthritis they have to get even a small job like that done by someone else & it always has cost at least a dollar.

I'm going to call a ticket agent about our trip tomorrow & then go & see them. Will tell you all about it the next time I write. Tues. nite Mom, Dad, & I started the invitations. We have finished most of them, but we ran out of those tissues so the printer is giving us more. All the invitations will be mailed Sat. Do you want me to send one to Al & Kay Keith?

When we got home last nite I wrote three letters, one to Diane, one to Lilly, & one to Doreen & Keith B.- at last! I was going to write you, too, but decided to wait & see if I would hear from you today.

Bob Griffin heard you were down to Toro. for the weekend & he called my place Tues, but I wasn't in. He hasn't called back yet. Have you taken any more pictures with the camera? I took our film in, but haven't been back to pick it up. I'll send you some prints if they turn out ok. Were you able to understand the little story I enclosed in my first letter? I forgot to ask you when you were here & I can't remember if you mentioned it.

Mom brought me back a smart ashtray from North Bay. It has a large shell in the centre & smaller ones all around it – the base is painted yellow & has N. Bay Ont printed on it.

They didn't say boo when I told them you had been down to Toro for the weekend. No kidding. They seemed glad. They didn't even say anything when I said that you & Russ & Pat had stayed Sun. nite. Mom said it was swell I had some company because I hate to stay alone. Isn't it funny when you expect the worst it never comes.

By the way, Dad & I were figuring for fun how much money the wedding is costing between my dress, the reception, flowers, cake & such. The staggering sum is $658 so far!

Well honey, it's getting late & I want to get to bed early. I love you very much. Please write soon.

All my love

Lois

My time for the wk is:

Sun.	Aug. 9	10 – 1:30	6:30 – 10
Mon.	Aug. 10	7 – 4	
Tues.	" 11	7 – 4	
Wed.	" 12	12 – 8	
Thurs.	" 13	6 – 12	
Fri.	" 14	OFF	
Sat.	" 15	OFF	
Sun.	" 16	OFF	

A staggering sum indeed! $658.00 was a lot of money in 1953. Seems they were sparing no expense.

****

Mom really did hate being alone. She had never lived on her own, never even had her own bedroom, and after Dad died, her biggest concern was whether or not she could stay in the condo all by herself. Physically, she could, with support for some of the housework. It was the emotional side of it that was dicey. She spent the first week after Dad's death at my sister's home, and we talked about whether she wanted to live with one of us. In the end, she decided to give the single life a try, and see how she felt about it. She most definitely did not want to live in "one of THOSE places" as she referred to assisted living apartments.

She felt sad and lonely at first. Her sister, Barb, came down to visit with her. My sister dropped in for lunch every Monday when she commuted to the city for work, and also visited her nearly every weekend. Mom always had a long list of things she wanted done on those weekend visits. I lived too far away to visit with anything like regularity, and the Covid-19 crisis was still in full swing. Travel out of my region was restricted at one point unless we wanted to quarantine the whole household upon my return and my son's work and school schedule made that really impractical, but we talked on the phone frequently. After the initial settling in period, we thought Mom was doing well. She was full of plans for redecorating, had discovered online shopping (and was an instant devotee), and she had a solid group of friends in the condo with whom she visited or talked to daily. Several of them ran errands for her, including grocery shopping. But she missed Dad terribly, and as the anniversary of his death approached, she struggled emotionally again.

Mr & Mrs K Baggaley
Box 31
Clinton Ont

I have already written them

Lois.

That's all that was in this one envelope.

Mrs. Parker's Bird

Aug. 7/53

Dear Bill,

Here it is Fri. nite. I'm all alone & very lonely. I'd give almost anything to have you with me. I received a letter from you today. I think it's swell that you finally got a radio. We are looking after Mrs. Parker's bird while they are out west. It's nearly as bad as the dog. When I came home from work tonite the bird started singing & of course the dog started yelping. I had a rare time trying to quiet them.

The ticket agent has started to work on our trip. We had to give them a $10 deposit before they could start. The people who arranged Mom's trip to California are doing it for us. Their name is Calladine & Baldry. You've probably noticed their place. It's on Broadview just below Gerrard. They are very good so we have nothing to worry about. Please excuse the sloppy writing. I'm lying here in the Lazy Boy. I haven't much more to tell you except that I am sending you a small parcel tomorrow. Make sure to ask about it if you don't get it sometime next wk.

I'll close now honey.

I love you.

Lois

In 1962, James Calladine, of the family travel agency Calladine & Baldry on Broadview Avenue in Toronto, sent a job offer to a keen young man, Dennis Gill, whom he'd met in London, England. Gill accepted the job, and eventually founded Suntours, for a long time Canada's largest tour operator.

*****

Radios used to be such a big deal. That's where the new music came from! Growing up in Toronto, we had a lot of stations to choose from, and as a young teenager, I discovered Q107, a station that at the time played new music, stuff that easily competed, at least for me, with the tired 70's rock (as good as some of it was) and the endless disco hits. Punk and new wave out of England. The Ramones. Deborah Harry. Elvis Costello. I stuck my small, transistor radio under the edge of my pillow and kept the volume low so my parents wouldn't hear it as I stayed up late calibrating my brain to new sounds.

The Whole Afternoon Off

Aug. 9/53

"At Work"

Dear Bill,

I have the whole afternoon off so thought I'd drop you a line. Am enclosing the pictures we took. They aren't too bad. Could have been a little better. How do you like the one of "wide eyes" sitting in the bedroom? Also dead eye dick in the living room? Our engagement notice was in Sat. nite's Star. Will send you a clipping in my next letter. We received our first wedding gift yesterday – from Mr. & Mrs. Kneen – a G.E. automatic featherweight iron. Nice, heh? All the invitations have been mailed now so I guess we can expect a lot more parcels. I wish you could be here to help open them. It's fun. Just like Christmas! Just thirteen more dreary days & you will be back. I can hardly wait. 27 days till the wedding now. It's hard to believe isn't it?

I was thinking that when you come back, you should move into the apartment. Then you wouldn't have to be paying board at home. We could move things in before you come home as long as the painters are finished. I have dishes, etc. The studio couch chair & the kitchen &

furniture would be all you'd need. We have an old kettle & iron & such at our place that you could use. It would be cheaper than paying $20 board & $15 a wk. for the apt. even when you figure the food. You will be at my place a great majority of the time anyway. What do you think? I guess you'd rather not though. Just an idea.

I mailed that parcel Sat. so don't forget to ask about it if it isn't there by the end of this week.

When I visited Jean on Thurs. I saw their living room with its new paint. Surprise! It actually does look nice. The room looks much bigger & the buff trim gives it a modern touch. Nicer than I expected. Larry is really walking now. He looks like a drunk, though – wobbles all around the room.

Am going to the shower for Pat this Fri. Received an invitation in the mail last Fri.

The photographer who did Marilyn's wedding has a picture of Lynn, Shirley Ann & I in the window of his studio. Haven't seen it yet, but Lynn says it's very good.

Did you mention anything to the office about coming home the 15th? I don't suppose they will ever let you. Well, dear, I guess I'll go upstairs & sleep for a while.

All my love

Lois

This is the only letter that was written in pencil instead of ink. These pictures were not with that particular letter; they were in a separate envelope at the bottom of the pile, but they would be around the right time period and sure sound like the pictures she mentions. The picture of Dad was probably taken inside my grandparents' home in Parkview Hills. What jumped out at me was that Dad was wearing his shoes in the house! I can't imagine that being okay, but there you have it.

*****

Paying only $15 a week for an apartment in Toronto sounds like a wild fantasy! Even considering an average weekly wage of only $70 (for men in 1956), that was still only between 20-25% of earnings.

Average weekly earnings in Canada now are just over $1000 a week, so call it $4000 a month, but a one-bedroom apartment in Toronto is easily $1800 a month, which is 45% of one's earnings, edging towards 50% lately, as $1800 is at the low end.

Waist: 22"

Aug. 11/53

Dear Bill,

Was so pleased at last to receive a nice, lengthy letter from you. The joke was very cute. I'm enclosing a copy of our engagement notice. Please keep it as it's the only one I have. I worked 7 – 4 today & came home with very good intentions of washing my hair, taking a bath & going to bed, but Mrs. Corcoran called to say the first coat of paint was on the rooms & the painter wants me to go down tonite. All the rooms in the apt. have doors. Don't you remember? The only one we weren't sure about was the kitchen. I don't think I'll send Kay & Al an invitation. I'm sorry I forgot to send my measurements. I really don't think you should spend any money on anything for me, no matter if it costs even a little. Anyway, here they are: (don't laugh)

WAIST: 22" – which is size 12

BUST: 34" – which is size 14

HIPS: 34" – which is size 14

Is that all you want? (hmmm)

Alma Allen came up last nite (you know – the woman who can't hear). She brought me a gift – not a wedding gift – a shower gift if you please. She said she bought it for me & then didn't get invited to any of my showers.

It is a crystal water decanter with a glass to match – done in the cornflower pattern. They aren't too big. Just the right size to keep beside the bed. I have to eat supper now. Will continue later . . . . . .

<u>10:30 PM</u> Barby & I just came home from Corcorans. The rooms look terrific. Just what we wanted dear. They are going to clean all the hardwood floors for us & have the woodwork in the living room freshly varnished. The woodwork in the bedroom is all blue. The bedroom really looks nice. It is very pale blue right now but the second coat will darken it down just right – I think – I hope.

You mentioned in your letter that you wouldn't be coming home till the 23rd. I thought it was to be the 22nd. Can't you leave Fri. the 21st at nite & arrive in Toro. Sat.? Just 11 more days, honey. I'll be so happy to see you. Be sure to let me know exactly what time you're arriving back so I can come & meet you. I don't care what time it is. I'm closing now dear. I love you very much.

Lois

MR. AND MRS. EDWARD L. FORTH announce the engagement of their daughter, Lois Viola, to Herbert William Long, son of Mr. and Mrs. Percival Long. The marriage will take place on Saturday, September 5, at 7 o'clock, in St. John's Anglican church (Norway).

Picturing Mom with a 22 inch waist is just not easy. If we didn't have the photos to prove it, I would have been sure she'd been exaggerating how thin she was. I remember Mom being unhappy with her body. She tried exercises and diets from time to time, but I think she eventually gave up and accepted, to some degree, her size. Her weight affected her knees adversely, though. She eventually had knee surgery in her seventies after years of debilitating pain and reduced mobility. She was so happy to be able to walk pain-free for the first time in ages. Then she slipped on the back deck at my sister's house, fell, and broke her femur pretty badly. Months of recovery ensued, including a summer-long stint in one of "THOSE places" (a long-term care facility) until she could get mobile again. Dad visited every day for hours. She healed pretty well, given how bad the break was, but she was afraid of falling again, and used a walker consistently afterwards, even just to get around in the condo.

Still Haven't Washed My Hair

Aug. 13/53

Dear Bill,

Received your letter this morning & am happy to hear the parcel arrived okay. I'm so pleased you like it. It didn't cost very much, but I knew you wanted one. I think I got as big a kick from buying it as you did when you got it.

I'm 6 – 12 today. Still haven't washed my hair so am going to try to do so before I go to work.

When are you going to send me a sample of your poetry? I'm very interested.

We will be using Mom's studio couch instead of Kay's. Also, Mom's armchair. She washed the slipcover on the chair & it really looks nice. It has maroon, grey & green in it so should look ok in <u>our</u> living room. We will only need a slipcover for the studio couch now.

You <u>will</u> be coming home on <u>Sat.</u> morning will you dear? I miss you so much. It will be wonderful to have you back again.

We have started to receive answers to our invitations. Vi & Alec will be coming. They are the only ones I've heard from on your side of the family. But we know Lilly & Gord are coming anyway.

Am glad you like the pictures. Have you any to send me from Montreal?

I haven't been talking to Al's wife since the weekend you came down. I <u>have</u> been very busy though, shopping & such. It wouldn't hurt her to call me. When do they have to be out of their apt.?

<u>11:10 AM</u> Just had time out for breakfast. I don't feel very good today. Last nite I couldn't sleep although I felt very tired. It's an awful feeling. I'm not sure, but I think I've lost <u>more</u> weight. Of course, I'm not <u>trying</u> to lose because if I get any thinner I'll look terrible. The suit I bought is a size 12. They let it down & took it out a little in the hips, but that's all they had to do. Just call me beanpole! For short.

Well, Kay just came in & she is busy talking a mile a minute. Also, I'm running out of decent writing paper, so I'll close now.

All my love

Lois

Dad wrote POETRY??!!! I'd give anything to see one of his poems. But all I have is one of their wedding invitations I found with their wedding album.

Mr. and Mrs. Edward Forth
request the honour of your presence
at the marriage of their daughter

Lois Viola
to

Herbert William Long
on Saturday, September the fifth
nineteen hundred and fifty-three
at seven o'clock

St. Johns Anglican Church, Norway
Kingston Road at Woodbine

Reception at
Prince Arthur House
145 St. George Street   R.S.V.P

You Can Bet Your Life

Aug. 14/53

Dear Bill,

Just came home from the shower for Pat. She was very surprised & received some lovely things. Your letter came this morning & I'm so happy you're coming home Sat. I was supposed to work, but one of the girls said she would work for me. You can bet your life I'll be at the station to meet you, honey. Oh boy! I can hardly wait! This is positively the last time I want you to go away for this long again. If they want to send you again (other than when you will go out on the road) I'm going too – so help me!

We received another gift today – from Alma Allen – a Scotch lace tablecloth.

Well dear, I still think it would save money if you moved into the apt. when you came back, Mom says you will probably be eating here most of the time anyway. I can't see why it wouldn't save money, but if you're not interested – <u>okay</u> (I still disagree). Enough of that. I want to mail this tonite so will close now. I love you, honey.

Lois

Mom and Dad could both be stubborn in their own ways, but I think Mom edged out Dad for the first prize in that category. He was wise to come back on the Saturday.

Mom was so honest about her infatuation. She didn't play it cool. All her cards were on the table in plain sight with nothing up her sleeve. I ran this book by my Aunt Barbara before publishing it, and she was fairly stunned by just how much Mom had been dwelling on the relationship with Dad at the time. "I knew she was in love," she said, "but I had no idea just how completely consumed she was." My aunt remembers those teenage years as being years of friendships with both girls and boys, nothing as serious as the letters reveal.

That Mom and Dad loved each other was never in question, even when they had loud disagreements. "We're not fighting," my Mom would say. "We're just having an active discussion."

I knew they'd married young, but before I read these letters, I'm not sure I fully understood the depth of that emotional bond.

Don't Shoot Me!

Aug. 17/53

Dear Bill,

Received your postcard today. Quite the thing! I've never seen any like it before. It was a nice surprise to get your phone call Sat. nite.

It's funny, I can never think of a thing to say when you phone me, but can always talk when I see you.

I sent Kay & Al's invitation Sun. so they should have it by now. Don & Jean want us to go down to visit them the day after you come back (Sun.). I told them we would let them know.

I hope you let your parents know you'll be back Sat. You really should. (I guess?)

This week is going to go very slow for me. It will probably seem like five more years instead of days. Don't shoot me! But I still haven't taken our marriage licence to the minister yet, but am going to do it this wk before you come back. Honest!

Mom & Dad have gone out. I told Mom I'd wash the dishes so I better get a move on. Let's see now, you will get this letter Thurs. & then it will only be <u>1 more day</u> & you'll be home (not anxious or anything, am I?) Will see you soon dear.

All my love

Lois

P.S. excuse lopsided writing – writ by hand on the couch

Mom and Dad were married in St. John's Anglican Church Norway at Woodbine Avenue and Kingston Road in Toronto on September 5, 1953. I found this clipping in a photo album.

LONG—FORTH

At a candlelight service in St. John's Anglican church, Norway, the marriage was solemnized by Rev. J. F. O'Neil, of Lois Forth, daughter of Mr. and Mrs. Edward L. Forth, to William Long, son of Mr. and Mrs. Percival Long. Given away by her father, the bride wore a gown of white satin and nylon tulle, fashioned with fitted bodice of Chantilly lace and a tulle yoke. A double flounce of the lace fell over a full skirt of tulle and satin, and her veil of tulle illusion was caught to a small hat. She carried white 'mums and stephanotis. Matron of honor Mrs. Jean McCabe, and Barbara Forth and Diane Swan, bridesmaids, wore peach, bronze and green taffeta with bandeaux of flowers to match their bouquets of peach gladioli and bronze 'mums. Nikki Kalpakis was flower girl frocked in yellow taffeta. Russel Dyson was best man and ushers were Alfred Orchard and Donald McCabe. The bride's mother received in a brown taffeta coat-dress with corsage of yellow roses, assisted by the groom's mother wearing a navy and white ensemble with red roses.

Lois and Bill spent every day in each other's company for the next 66 years until my Dad's death from lung cancer in June of 2020. Mom was lost without him. She died in July of 2021, technically of an infection, but we suspect she just didn't feel like carrying on without the love of her life by her side.

Between 1953 and 2020, they lived well, and left three grandchildren in this world who have no doubts about how much Grandma and Grandpa adored them.

Not all teenage romances have happy endings. Theirs did. Here's to Lois and Bill – they never stopped loving each other.

Afterword

Finding Mom's letters allowed us a glimpse into the part of a parent's life to which one rarely has access. Neither Bill nor Lois achieved anything approximating fame in their lifetimes. Like billions of us, they grew up, worked, parented children, achieved some goals, and had to sacrifice others. They both lived well into their eighties, which is an achievement in itself. The one-sided correspondence that turned into Dear Bill could be thought of as an extended obituary, I suppose. For me, it was a grief project, a way to come to terms with the death of both of them in such a short time span during the Covid-19 wave, which restricted how often I could see them in their last two years of life. Especially heartbreaking was the small window of time I was allowed to spend with Mom each day while she was in the hospital.

We miss them. My sister, me, my cousins, and all who knew them. Their marriage had its ups and downs. What marriage doesn't? But they were one of those couples that make you believe that if you just find the right person, there really is a "happily ever after". Well, sometimes happily. Sometimes it's just an "ever after" and you wonder if you did the right thing.

After I transcribed the 50's letters, my sister found one more in a random box of Dad's things and emailed it to me. It was dated November of 1974, and chronicles one of the low points in their marriage.

I remember that time period vividly. I recall feeling unsettled, anxious, as if something were wrong and I couldn't define it. I asked my Dad, "Why does it feel like everything's changing?" and he gave me one of his famously vague responses along the lines of, "Oh, we're just going through some things right now." It was a deeply unsatisfying answer to my question, but I knew I wasn't going to get any more out of him.

My sister was younger, and says she doesn't have any memories of that specific time, but she does have a later one that connects to its aftermath. She said in her email to me,

> "I think they went deeply into debt to pay for those things. I remember her once blowing up about something when I was a teenager and saying 'We have business debts that you wouldn't believe!'. She was so worked up about it, it stuck with me all these years."

In her letter, Mom refers to opening up the back of the house by removing a window in the dining room, and replacing it with a set of sliding glass doors that opened onto a deck, a huge improvement to the living space. Shortly after she wrote it, more renovations happened. We got new furniture, including a dining room set. The kitchen received a makeover. We also started taking family vacations – Florida and the U.S. Virgin Islands stand out for me - but the biggest change in our lives was the swimming pool. Mom and Dad first had a circular above-ground pool, and then a full in-ground pool installed. It's a good thing she let him read the letter. Sounds like it might have saved their marriage at the time. And we got a pool out of it, so I can't complain.

Nov. 28, 1974

Dear Bill,

This morning you said the communication is up to me. You are right. I have tried all week to talk but each time I try to talk "face to face" I can't, because I know I will, in typical female fashion, cry.

Last Friday night I "turned off" & even though I've tried, I can't "turn on". The disagreement seemed to trigger a whole chain of thinking that I can't shove aside. The following are some of my thoughts.

I am unhappy. Why?

I don't like what our life has become.

Our home should be a refuge for all of us. It is, instead, chaos. Disorder & confusion exists nearly all the time. We are doing very little together to make our house a true home. It needs love & attention. These cost both time & money. I wonder, if the feeling was there – if the time & money wouldn't be found just as it is found for other things when we really want them.

It would be nice to have some social life in our own home. A party to celebrate our deck and doors would have been nice, but how could we? A Christmas Party or an Open House would be great, but again how could we? Take a good, long, serious look around our house. We have no home, just a collection of half-finished things. I can't even invite a neighbour in to sit down on a decent piece of furniture or invite friends in to dinner. I feel these things stronger than you because I spend more time in our house than you. You can escape from it with your work.

We all have physical, emotional, & material needs. Until this past week I think we were taking good care of our physical needs & in part our emotional needs. Material needs differ, or at least ours seem to differ. To take care of some of my emotional needs, I need material things – comfortable surroundings are important to me & and are needed to make a home. We never seem to have the spare time or money to provide for material needs. Each time there is any extra money we have to buy something for the business or pay a business debt.

The Business – is it worth it?

I have a strong feeling that our business is costing me all I hold dear in life – you & me, our children, our home. I have tried telling myself, "Never mind, Lois – next year things will be better. Onward & upward. We will have a better life for ourselves soon." It didn't work.

I know that next year – if we have any extra money – it will have to be used for our business – another car – a full time employee – perhaps another office move & the business wins again. We don't seem to make enough from it to compensate for all the time & energy devoted to it.

To me the business has become a continuing drain – financially, physically & emotionally.

Yet a while ago you told me you were still happy having the business. I thought if you were happy then I could be happy – not so! It is winning. We are losing each other.

Do we Love each other?

I know I love you. That is the one thing I am sure of & that is the love I have for you. It is not just a "sexual thing". My love for you has deepened over the past 21 years. I suppose that's why I'm writing my thoughts down for you. If my love is reciprocated then it's worth keeping & worth working hard – even fighting to keep.

I have also asked myself – Isn't love all that matters? Doesn't love conquer all? If that's true, then something is very, very wrong. Maybe we don't love enough – if so we would be more sensitive to each other's needs – physical, emotional, & material. Do we honestly try?

The answers?

I have none – and rightly so. A marriage is two people & communication. If we can't communicate face to face then we are nowhere. Perhaps now this is "off my chest" we can talk – not argue & yell, talk sensibly.

My last thought – Should I leave? You probably think I'm the perfect candidate for the nearest "funny farm" anyway after reading all this. Believe me, writing it down has helped & I even considered not letting you read this but decided that wouldn't be right. I would like to do something the right way for a change.

I keep thinking if you are content to live the way we've been living then I should be the one to leave. The children are reasonably happy. I only know I can't live here with things the way they are. If I try I will hurt you & the girls & you are the ones I love most.

L.

My sister and I have no idea what Mom would have done if she'd left, where she would have gone, how she would have supported herself. That she was even thinking about leaving the marriage must have thrown my Dad into a panic. Although Mom stars as the love-struck protagonist of this story, Dad was no less in love with her, and if we had even one of his letters, I'm sure that would be obvious. One thing didn't change. Despite all the new furniture and the pool, Mom and Dad didn't throw big parties or have lots of friends over. As far as we could tell, they had very little need or desire for company beyond that of each other. They socialized regularly with the parents of one of my childhood friends, and a neighbour couple, and that was about it.

Mom was probably happier, though, having those material comforts that were so important to her, and her happiness would have made Dad happy, too. Crisis averted. Marriage intact. Bring on the children's teenaged years – but that's a whole different book.

The letters my Mom wrote are completely unedited with one exception. She copied out the entire lyrics to Jo Stafford's song, "You Belong To Me". Because there was a question of copyright infringement, and because licensing fees are exorbitant, I decided to leave those out.

I want to thank all the people I pestered for photos or photo permissions. Shout out to Kristina Woodcock, in particular, for the train photo, and to Richard Woodcock for his helpful memories of Kirkland Lake in past decades. I'm grateful to my cousin, Beverley Wills, for the photo of Mom's engagement ring. Thanks to Eliza

Moore for helping me with my research. Aaron Burden and Megan Lee get credit for the photos of the fountain pen and the teacup on the front cover. Stewart Kramer at PARS International deserves thanks for his infinite patience with me as I tried to navigate the process for obtaining permission to re-print Toronto Star material. Special thanks to my Aunt Barbara and my sister, Tracey, for their valuable insights and corrections, and to my husband, David, for his editing and helpful comments. Any remaining errors are my own.

Bibliography

Arcade Building (Toronto). *Wikipedia* https://en.wikipedia. org/wiki/Arcade_Building_(Toronto)

Arthur Lucas and Ronald Turpin. *Mount Pleasant Group* https://www.mountpleasantgroup.com/en-CA/General-Information/Our-Monthly-Story/story-archives/prospect-cemetery/Lucas.aspx

Average earnings of male and female employees in manufacturing, survey week 1956 to 1965, and percentage increases over previous year. *Statistics Canada.* https://www65.statcan.gc.ca/acyb02/1967/ acyb02_19670756015-eng.htm

Average weekly wages and salaries, industrial composite, by province, 1939 to 1975. *Statistics Canada Archives.* https://www150.statcan.gc.ca/n1/pub/11-516-x/ sectione/4147438-eng.htm

Bishop, Mary F. History of Birth Control in Canada. (2021). *The Canadian Encyclopedia.* https://www.the canadianencyclopedia.ca/en/article/history-of-birth-control-in-canada

Bradburn, Jamie. (2009). Historicist: The Rise and Fall of a Shopping Arcade. *The Torontoist.* https://torontoist. com/2009/03/historicist_the_rise_and_fall_of_a/

Folster, David. (1982). You Can't Wire There From Here. *McLean's Magazine.* https://archive.macleans.ca/article/1982/4/19/you-cant-wire-there-from-here

Goldenberg, Susan. (2018). Where was Boyd Gang in September 1952? Hiding in North York, as it turns out. *North York Mirror.* https://nyhs.ca/where-was-boyd-gang-in-september-1952-hiding-in-north-york-as-it-turns-out/

Levine, Allan. (2014). *Toronto: Biography of a City.* Douglas and McIntyre

MacDonald, Sharon. (1998). The Bell Club: One Hundred Years of Women's Cultural and Literary Life in Baddeck, Nova Scotia. *Atlantis.* Vol. 20. No. 1. Pp. 49-62. https://journals.msvu.ca

Maurice Rocco. *WBSS Media.* https://wbssmedia.com/artists/detail/131

McIntyre, Catherine (2017). Why the swastika can't be rehabilitated. *Maclean's Magazine.* https://www.macleans.ca/news/why-the-swastika-cant-be-rehabilitated/

Nyhuis, Phillip. (2012, Updated 2020). WNY's All Time Greatest Nightclub: The Town Casino. *Buffalo Spree.* https://www.buffalospree.com/features/wnys-all-time-greatest-nightclub-the-town-casino/article_17b58d46-51ed-5a5e-b6be-4fa3e4c9d340.html

Raymond, Katrine. (2020). Mabel Hubbard Bell. *The Canadian Encyclopedia.* https://www.thecanadian encyclopedia.ca/en/article/mabel-hubbard-bell

Sherk, Sandra. (2018). How Did People Get By Before Credit Cards? *Credit Canada.* https://www.creditcanada. com/blog/how-did-people-get-by-before-credit-cards

Taylor, John D. (2016) Toronto's Yonge Street Arcade (demolished). *Historic Toronto.* https:// tayloronhistory.com/2016/07/29/torontos-yonge-street-arcade-demolished/

The Birth Control Pill: A History. (2015). *Planned Parenthood Federation of America.* https://www.planned parenthood.org/files/1514/3518/7100/Pill_History_ FactSheet.pdf

Thompson, John. (2017) Ontario Northland: Through timber to tidewater. *Railway Age.* https://www. railwayage.com/news/ontario-northland-through-timbe r-to-tidewater/

Young, Jeffery. (2006, updated 2015). Locomotives and Rolling Stock. *The Canadian Encyclopedia.* https://www.thecanadianencyclopedia.ca/en/article/ locomotives-and-rolling-stock

Zelasko, Ellen M. (2020) The Town Casino/The Town Ballroom. *Hello Buffalo.* https://hellobuffalohikes.com/ the-town-ballroom-the-town-casino/

About the Author

Photo credit: Jason McKenzie, Thunder Bay.

Cindy Long has been a freelance writer for decades, writing everything from snowmobile reviews to feature articles. She also writes radio and television ads. Her work has appeared in the Ottawa Citizen, and the Thunder Bay Chronicle-Journal, as well as several magazines.

Cindy was born in Toronto, and currently lives in Thunder Bay, Ontario with her husband, teenaged son, and a leopard gecko.

She's an avid nature nerd, and has spent a lot of time photographing insects and mushrooms. She also enjoys travelling, political debates, good movies, and excellent grilled cheese sandwiches. *Dear Bill* is her first book.

www.ingramcontent.com/pod-product-compliance
Lightning Source LLC
Chambersburg PA
CBHW051106050726
47592CB00002B/686